BEST OF THREE WORLDS

WITH A PILE OF ROTIS

A soulful, cultural and historical journey across three continents

---

Hansa Pankhania

Published by
Filament Publishing Ltd
16, Croydon Road, Waddon, Croydon,
Surrey, CR0 4PA, United Kingdom
Telephone +44 (0)20 8688 2598
Fax +44 (0)20 7183 7186
info@filamentpublishing.com
www.filamentpublishing.com

ISBN 978-1-912635-80-1.

Printed by IngramSpark

CONTENTS

FOREWORD

I really enjoyed reading these memoirs. The overriding impression I was left with, is that for the author, love, humanity and the idea that we are all part of a world family mean much more than national and cultural identity. That is a powerful and valuable message.

It is interesting that others were more fascinated by her multi-layered cultural identity than she was initially, maybe because most people do not have such a rich background. Perhaps it is the same with cultural identity, we just accept our own background as the norm, even though in some cases, like this, it might be quite special!

I loved the way the author talks about the one-mile world and ten-mile world of her childhood, and how, thanks to her parents, she had no sense of the disquiet in the wider world beyond, only learning about what was happening in Kenya much later through conversation with a friend. I loved reading about the courgette plant that covered the house and picking the mangoes. From the book, I had the impression that she very easily accepted the move to the UK, which surprised me. Leaving familiar home, friends, the glorious sunshine and the beauty of Kenya and moving to cold, grey, ugly Birmingham cannot have been easy!

The passages about her first trip to India and family holiday to Kenya are very descriptive and engaging, among the best parts of the book. I particularly enjoyed the evocative description of the trip to the cinema in India and reading about the reactions of her children on the Kenyan Holiday.

It strikes me that she has created a very personal cultural identity from her own recipe, perfected over the years.

This book is really thought-provoking. I very much enjoyed reading it and would have liked to read more.

– Sara Rowell, Solihull Writers' Group

PROLOGUE – BIRMINGHAM, WEST MIDLANDS, ENGLAND, 2017

I wake up and realise my equator sun of many years ago has crept into my dreams. The telephone rings, bringing me back to my present world. I jump up, grab the phone and mumble a sleepy *'Hello?'* to the caller. My new friend Katie wants to know what time I will go over to her house later that day.

That afternoon, I am relaxing at her house, enjoying an English cup of tea accompanied by an Indian snack. My mobile phone rings and I have a short conversation with my sister. When I get off the phone, Katie says,

'That was amazing. You were switching between English and some other language every sentence but still kept the flow of the conversation.'

'Really?' I respond. 'To me, that feels as natural as breathing.'

To which she asks, 'How come?'

'Well, I was brought up with three languages: English, Gujerati and Swahili,' I say.

'I know you speak English very well, so is Gu...je...rati one of the Indian regional languages? And Swahili is African, is it?'

I nod. 'Yes, Swahili is the national language of Kenya.'

My friend is silent for a few moments and the look in her eyes when she meets my gaze says she is very puzzled.

I think to myself, 'Here we go, yet again,' and I explain, 'I was born in the British Colony of Kenya.'

'So, how come your parents were in Kenya if they are Indian? How come you were born in Kenya, an African country? I hope you don't mind me asking but, obviously, you look very Indian and are living in England.'

She wants to know my story.

Katie was born in Manchester, moved to Birmingham in her teens and has had a handful of holidays abroad. She says she assumed I came to this country from India as an economic migrant.

I say, 'My parents were born in India as subjects of the British Empire. My dad and grandad sought work in the British Protectorate of East Africa, where present-day Kenya is. In the years following Kenyan independence, Indian-Kenyans began to feel less welcome in Kenya, so, as British passport-holders, my family moved to England.'

At that moment, our attention is drawn to the television as a heated debate on immigration is taking place as part of the Brexit issues. After listening for a few minutes to a right-wing politician talk about curbing immigration, we resume our robust conversation. She wants to know where my allegiance is and to which country. She wants to know who I am as a person with these diverse influences. She wants to know whether I will make my children marry an Indian, African or English person.

Towards the end of my visit, Katie says, 'Hansa, you have written other books, why don't you write a book on all this? I found our conversation today absolutely fascinating and want to know more.'

'Okay, I promise to think about it,' I say as we part for the evening. Another friend of mine, Jane, also said this to me many years ago.

For numerous days after, I reflect on who I am and what makes me who I am in light of the African, English and Indian imprints. What is my purpose, and do I have a legacy to leave for my future generations? It strikes me there is a risk that this rich cultural history and journey across three continents might never be known to the world. This story needs to be told. In light of the current conflict surrounding intercultural issues, I want the British people to understand that this Indian from Kenya and her future generations are as British as they are.

And that is how this book is born.

I am delighted to take the reader on an adventure that immerses them in the enchanting interrelationships between African culture and exposure to diversity from birth, the richness of Indian influences and living a simple life in tune with nature, and my western education in England and life in a democracy. In particular, I want to share my memories of a moment in time when an Indian-origin child born in the British Colony of Kenya witnesses the liberation of a new African nation. I hope I can convince the reader that 'Britishness' is nothing without its ties to the Commonwealth and therefore cultural variation need not be a threat to the concept of Britishness.

All through my life's journey, I have been enveloped with the love, acceptance, connectedness and humility I received from my parents, siblings and husband that I believe is a basic human need for safety and a sense of purpose and belonging. All this amidst the delicious sacred aroma of a pile of *rotis!* These influences have helped me to grow from a fearful little girl in a small town in Africa to a confident professional woman today – unafraid to be in the public eye and with a mission to help others be the best they can.

This is my journey as a Commonwealth subject, the product of three proud cultural identities each with a rich history. This is the story of how diversity can enrich our world and bring us together through the simple concept of humanity.

CHAPTER 1

THIKA, KIAMBU DISTRICT, KENYA 1958

My first memory as a child is of the hibiscus shrub looming high up over the tiny figure of my three-year-old self. I peer at a bright reddish bloom drooping from the green branch a few inches above me, touch the soft petal, and try to make sense of the other four similar petals in a circle. I am intrigued, drawn to the long thin bit sticking out from the middle of the circular shape, and notice it has some small spotty bits at the end. My tiny nimble fingers reach out, trying to grasp these, but they disintegrate at my touch. I hear myself letting out a muffled sound at the touch of the soft pollen on my hand. I rub it awkwardly to brush off the yellowy-pink residue from my hand which, instead of disappearing, leaves a small coloured shape on my tiny palm.

I raise my head, distracted by the large green carpet of lush green that goes beyond my low-cast horizon. Suddenly, I hear my name being called. Looking up I see my friend Sima beckoning me over to her. I run towards my friend; however, there is a big hole at my feet, brown, dusty and damp, extending all the way to my left and to my right too. Eager and excited to get to Sima, I try to step over the hole, but I stumble, roll and land at the bottom. A sharp sensation goes through my forehead, arms, legs and body faltering over my tiny head.

'*Baa…*' I shriek as I feel a stabbing throb somewhere on my face.

I have a blurred memory of a woman in bright clothing, her skin the colour of a glossy buttered chapatti, looking over me, and her muffled words fading away…

***

My next memory is of waking up in bed. 'Baa…' I call out, my tiny hand to my forehead.

'*Mane tukhe chhe,* (This is hurting), Baa…'

Next, I see Baa run up to me from the direction of the kitchen.

'You should look where you are going,' she says in a frustrated voice, but she makes reassuring noises and comforts and holds me with love.

I do not remember how long it took for the injury to heal but I have a memory of the loving attention from Baa and my siblings. This incident is permanently etched as a quarter-inch scar at the top-left of my forehead.

***

I am now five years old. It is quite normal in my childhood days to wander off to the green common, a large rectangular patch of grass and shrubs bordered by a road, houses and shops. The square is lined with a gutter about two feet wide and deep to gather the water from the surrounding area. Our house with the blue door is the second-to-last in a row, next to a lone fabric shop. The *Gurdwara* is round to the right corner and the *Mandir* directly opposite. A carpenter's workshop owned by our neighbours in the

2

last house stands beside the *Mandir*. There is a mill and another timber shop in the same row to the left. Baa and *Baapuji* know that if I am not in the house then they will find me in the grass square across the road where all the children from the neighbourhood gather to play.

The equator sun above is showing off today, shiny and bright like Baa's gold bangles. The pale-blue sky is reflected in the pastel shades of her cotton *saree*. There is the familiar earthy scent of the African soil in the air.

Children are having a game of *'Gili Danda'*. *Danda* is a makeshift bat and *gili* is a finger-length wooden oblong that Baapuji has made for us in his workshop. A bowler bowls the *gili* at the person batting. Fielders run or catch the *gili* before the batter gets to the stump ten or so yards away. I run up, dressed in my hand-me-down pink cotton dress and brown plastic shoes. I want to join in the game my brothers, sister and their friends are playing. I see *Bhai*, my older brother, bent to the right, both hands clutching the bat poised just above the ground. His gaze is fixed upon the *gili* being hurled towards him by his classmate who lives in the house on the opposite side of the green grass square.

'I want to bat. I want to bat.' I shout in my little voice, trying to get his attention.

'Not now, go away,' Bhai shouts, flicking his attention to me and missing the *gili* by a fraction of a second. 'Now look what you've made me do!'

After a fuss, the older children persuade me to sit with the three younger children playing *'Panchika'* in a corner away from the *Gili Danda* match. *Panchika* is a game played with five pebbles – *'panch'* means 'five' in Gujerati. You are seated and throw the *panchika* on the ground like you throw dice. Then you pick up one pebble and throw it in the air and catch it. You have to simultaneously pick the second pebble from the ground and catch the first one before it hits the ground. Holding on to the second you similarly pick up the third, fourth and fifth. If you miss any of them then you lose. The winner has to have all five pebbles in their palm without any of them falling on the ground. I try to compete with Sima and Niru but fail miserably. Niru has won the game and runs up excitedly to her sister who is a fielder in the *Gili Danda* match, making her miss a crucial catch. Some things never change – younger siblings being a nuisance and embarrassment to their older siblings!

A couple of hours later, Baa appears from the doorway of our house. She is looking beautiful in her sky-blue *saree* bordered with little daisy-shaped burgundy flowers. Her stature is lean and fragile but carrying a quiet strength about it at the same time. Her left arm sweeps her *saree* over her right shoulder to stop it slipping down as she calls out to all the children. It is nearly dusk and it is time for *Aarti* at the *Mandir* on the other side of the square. There is much clamour at having to leave the game unfinished, but Baa says if we get there first then we may have a chance of ringing the bells tonight.

A commotion follows and there is a race between all of us to get to the *Mandir*. I do not stand a chance as my older brothers make it there first. I follow with my little steps holding Baa's hand, feeling safe with the feel of her warm, soft fingers curled around mine in a firm grip. Sima and Niru trot beside me. Today their Baa is not coming but they know they are safe because it is known that they will be accompanied by any parent or one of the older siblings from the seven families living on either side of the square.

As I set foot into the temple, the scent of sandalwood from the incense animates my senses. I feel in awe of the three deities in bright orange attire placed on the altar at the far end of the temple, beyond the worshippers' platform. To my innocent eyes they are real living beings. I am told by Baa that they are there to look after me and my family, someone I can call on whenever there is confusion in my little world. I start a mental dialogue with the female deity who appears kind and approachable from the twinkle in her eyes and friendly smile. I ask her how she can help me so my brothers let me play *Gili Danda* with them tomorrow. I am just about to ask her how I win a game of *Panchika* when my mental chatter is halted.

The temple comes alive with the hypnotic sound of a conch shell that the *Maharaj* has put to his mouth and the chiming of bells rung by volunteers on either side of the deities. Today it is Bhai and his friend on one side and Niru and her sister on the other. The bells ring to the rhythm of the accompanying hymn-singing led by the *Maharaj* and supported by the worshipers of the *Aarti* ritual. My eyes follow the light of the lamp as the *Maharaj* circles it around the deity. My ears trail the melodious tunes coming from Baa. I look up and try to watch her lips match with the lyrics of the hymn, joining in with the odd word here and there. She looks down at me with tranquil eyes, smiles, and carries on with the singing and clapping – her gaze upon the deity expresses her complete and unflinching love for God. Slowly, all my troubles from the playground are diffused by this safe, magic world of light, colour and healing sounds. The *Maharaj* turns around and circles the lamp towards all the devotees as the ritual comes to the end. Baa whispers to me that this signifies everyone has a part of God within them.

One day enfolds into another.

It is literally a carefree and innocent existence as a child. We have a radio but no television in our house. Time after school, weekends, and holidays is spent playing outside with whichever children are there at that time. We do not have expensive toys so we make our own. My favourite is when my brothers give me rides on one of their homemade carts – four wheels attached to the underside of a two-by-one foot wooden plank. I sit on the plank and they push me until the wheels whisk me away, and then push me again when the cart comes to a halt. I squeal with delight and fright at the same time.

CHAPTER 2

ROTIS ROLLED IN DIVINE LOVE

THIKA, KENYA, 1962

I am two years older now and it's an after-school afternoon. We play in the grass square for a while and are enticed by the big mango and tamarind trees to the right of the temple area. Niru, Sima and I go walk-a-about. We cross the road and quietly sneak through the gates, making sure the *Maharaj* or his family members who live in the adjoining building do not see us. We have made it to the rows of huge mango trees and the smaller line of tamarind trees. We pick up stones and throw them at the shiny green mangoes, hoping to hit a few and for them to fall to the ground. My friends attempt the mangoes while I, being the smallest of the three, go for the pods of tamarind lower down. I grab a few pods and tie them into my handkerchief which Baa has pinned to the front of my frock.

'Yaaa...I got one,' screams Niru, and a minute later, so does Sima. Pleased with our efforts, we prepare to make our way back when we hear a man shouting in Swahili, 'You naughty girls, get away from the mango trees!' It's Kamangi, the *Maharaj's* gardener. He is coming our way. He quickens his steps as we shriek and bolt towards the gate. Niru stumbles on her knee, picks herself up, and we all aim for the gates. It feels as if we are running for our lives, but in the end later realise it is just for three unripe mangoes and two pods of tamarind. We just make it outside as he jams the gates shut, laughing to himself.

'*Asante sana* (Thank you very much), Kamangi,' we squeal in unison.

'Make sure you tell your mothers how many you helped yourselves to,' he shouts back in Swahili.

'*Ndiyo, Ndiyo* (Yes, Yes),' we reply in chorus and run towards Niru's house.

'What's the matter?' Niru's Baa exclaims at the sight of three frightened little girls escaping from the throes of grave danger and getting to safety. 'And what have you done to your knee?' she says as she spots the big bruise on Niru's knee.

She swiftly makes a paste of turmeric, salt, and water and smears it on Niru's knee before bandaging it with a clean cotton strip ripped from an old garment. My eyes drift to the yellow powder in the bottle next to her.

'Baa put a spoonful of that in milk, boiled it, and made Bhai drink it when he had a bad cough,' I say.

'But when my Bhai had a cold, my Baa boiled those brown and black things in jaggery,' Sima quips in.

'You are both right,' Niru's Baa says. 'Turmeric boiled in milk is good for getting rid of coughs, and cinnamon and cloves are good for overcoming a cold. Everybody has different levels of heat and coolness in their bodies. When the cold is excessive, we can balance it out with foods that instil heat, like cloves.' This goes well beyond the capacity of our little brains to understand, distracted as we are by a song on the radio in the next room sung by our favourite singer, Lata Mangeshkar. We run through and listen to the radio in earnest.

Half an hour later, we are sat in a circle still at Niru's house relishing the mango and tamarind that her Baa has chopped for us and sprinkled with salt and a little chili powder. She will have a word with the *Maharaj* tomorrow and make a small donation to the temple towards the mangoes. This is how our close-knit community works, where little childhood pranks and misdoings like these just take care of themselves.

It is only five o'clock in the afternoon and Baa will not expect me home until dusk. Niru's Baa invites us to help her make the dough for the evening meal's *rotis*. We wash our hands and scramble to the kitchen where we perch ourselves on the row of *patlas* laid out for us. In the deep aluminium *saani*, Niru pours the water into the well she has made in the middle of the heap of flour. Sima attempts to mix the water into the flour with a long wooden spoon. I get to mix it with my hands! My nimble fingers have a go at binding the two together, spilling a copious amount on the floor.

'Let me do it. I can do this better,' Niru says. Sima wants to have a go as well.

'Let her do it,' insists Niru's Baa as she intervenes gently, not wanting all the flour to end up on the floor. 'You will all learn to do this.'

Niru's Baa explains as she enfolds the ingredients, 'As you mix the flour and water, caress one with the other and infuse them with love. As you knead the dough, bind it with blessings. Do this for the people who will eat them so you feed their hearts as well as their bellies. Niru, you can knead the dough tomorrow, and Sima can do it when she comes to play on Saturday.'

We wash our hands and file back into the yard. As we do this, I think of Baa singing her *mantras* as she binds and kneads the dough for tonight's meal.

I start to hum the tune I have heard on the radio today but the lyrics do not fit together. Niru and Sima try to help. We attempt to fit the words to the tune and sing after each other.

'Aap ki... nazarone... samja, pyar ke... kabil muje.' (Your eyes say I am worthy of your love)

'This is hard – I can't do it. I listen more to the English radio station, and not like crazy to Lata Mangeshkar like you two,' Sima protests. 'Let's try "The Young Ones" by Cliff Richard.'

We all jump up to dance and sing, some parts in tune and some way out of scale.

'The young ones, darling we're the young ones.'

Sima does not like this one either so we join hands in a circle and resort to singing – *'Ringa, ringa roses, pocket full of posies.'*

The evening flies by... and it's the next morning in the playground at Shah Primary School, which is named after M. P. Shah, the main sponsor of the state school. Amongst the tittle-tattle of seven-year-olds you hear a group of girls in their khaki skirts and white blouses running and singing in a circle – *'Aitishooo, aitishooo, we all fall down.'*

Giggles and laughter follow as their delicate hands and legs stumble on to the grassy ground. They get up and ringa-roses again.

Mrs. Ajita appears, the purple of her *salwar kameez* standing out amongst the khaki and whites of the children, her cream arms signalling the end of play-time. We file back into the classroom and to our desks. We are sitting in order of our performance in class. I came Fourth in my times-tables recital and English readings, so I am paired up with Navin who came Third, just behind Raju who placed First and Sukhi, Second. Our teacher hands out books to the boys and girls.

It is an English lesson now and we practice our reading. Mrs. Ajita patiently guides us to make sense of the words on the blackboard and in our reading books before we stand up in turn and read before the class. I get a warm feeling inside of me when she pats me lightly on my back with a *'Well done'* after I finish my reading. This warm feeling is short-lived, however, as I get a snide comment from a boy in the last row. He has been having English tuition from Mrs. Rushtom, one of the teachers, but still did not manage to read accurately. He is one of the rich kids from Section Nine of the town, the rich kids who I perceived exuded a sense of superiority over we working-class bunch who lived by the temple area.

This is another stab into my self-esteem that slitters into my subconscious. The first one was when he made a false accusation against me a month ago. A teaching aid had been misplaced in class and he decided to put the blame on me because I was not as affluent as him. Being brought to the front of class to protest my innocence, rears its tentacles from the hidden corners of my psyche at times like this. I turn around to face him and he sneers down at my brown plastic shoes with a broken buckle. Another stab! I choose to ignore him for the rest of the day and sail through the Maths and Gujerati lessons.

I am in no mad rush to get home after mid-morning lessons. It is not lunchtime, so Baa is not expecting me to rush home before the afternoon session. I stroll through the narrow stone corridors towards the gate and pass by the big sign, SHAH PRIMARY SCHOOL. To my left is a free-standing house where the head teacher and his family live. Other children rush past me in the usual commotion. My classmate Jyot brushes past. She is stocky and quite a few inches taller than me. I hear her husky voice say to me,

'Shall we grab some *mogo*? I've got a *sumuni*.'

'Hmmm, got no money on me but would love some,' I say as I match my footsteps with hers.

We run up to Kamau, the street vendor outside the school gates. He is tall, skinny, with bright eyes shining in an oblong chocolate face. His generous lips grin as we approach his makeshift barbecue. To his left is a row of *mogo* slices roasting above the red and orange of the hot coals beneath the steel mesh. On his right is a row of cobs of corn crackling away to the rhythm of the sweltering coals underneath. He turns a few slices with his tongs, his brown fingers long and deft.

'*Jambo mtoto, rafiki,* (Hello, my little friends),' he greets us cheerily.

'*Jambo sana, Kamau,*' we giggle back. 'Two pieces please,' Jyot asks in Swahili and hands over the *sumuni.*

Kamau picks up two slices and makes a slit in the middle, sprinkling a mixture of salt and chilli powder into them.

'Limau? (Lemon),' he asks

'Kidogo, (A little),' Jyot nods to him.

He wraps up the slices in pieces of old newspaper and hands one to each of us.

'*Kwaheri* (Bye Bye).'

Jyot and I grab our *mogo* and run up to a stone ledge nearby where we perch ourselves and savour the hot snack. Then we run back to the water fountain in the school grounds to quench the burning taste of the hot *mogo* and chilli in our mouths. When I am given a *sumuni* by my *Fai* when she next visits, I shall treat Jyot to *mogo* or *banta pipi* (aniseed sweets) from the shop around the corner.

***

During the lunch break I walk at a brisk pace with a few friends or my older siblings to home half a mile away. As I set foot in the house, Baa's soft rendition of mantras sanctifies the ambience. I see Baa is cooking in the kitchen over her coal *sagdi* and the aroma of garlic and turmeric incites my hunger. In addition, the whiff of *rotis* cooking makes it heavenly. My siblings and I sit in a circle on *patlas* laid out on the kitchen floor, ready for Baa's sacred offering of the day.

We grow up nourished by a simple low-budget, mostly plant-based vegetarian diet passed down through generations. Baa says food is medicine to the body. She says bananas and okra are cooling to the body and balance out the heat from the effect of our equator sun. Baa says we should give gratitude and respect to everyone in the food chain, farmer, distributor, seller, cook, who make it possible for every single morsel that we devour.

Jerome does a house-to-house drop to all of the Baas on the street to sell his home-grown *bhoga*, and a bargaining slanging match always ensues. As well as bananas and the okra, Baapuji's favourite, she also buys *turiya*, aubergine, peas, tomatoes, guava and fresh fenugreek. Baa did not ever have to buy courgettes, though – Baa grew her own.

The courgette plant started from a four-foot-square mini allotment outside the kitchen wall and spread up our neighbour's garden wall and out over the roof of our house. There are courgettes galore of all sizes spread across the kitchen roof and the roof of the two adjoining rooms. There are enough courgettes to pass onto the neighbouring Baas. The other day Baa asked me to take an overgrown courgette to Niru's Baa to use as a bath loofah once it had dried out. It is not normal practice to pop into a shop for such household items – the community takes care of these needs.

Lunch is a big pile of *rotis*. Actually, breakfast is also a big pile of *rotis*, and supper a big pile of *rotis*. Well, it is really not as boring as it sounds. Breakfast is a pile of *rotis* with tea and sometimes pickles, lunch is a pile of *rotis* with a vegetable curry, and supper is a pile of *rotis* with yogurt or lentil soup, except for Sunday when it would be *khichadi*. Today, Baa scoops up cauliflower and pea curry onto our plates one by one. She is running late so there is only the beginning of a pile of *rotis*. If there was a big pile, we would help ourselves to what we wanted, but today she serves half of the *rotis* in turn so we can all begin to dowse our hunger.

She frantically rolls up one *roti* and drops it onto the hot griddle. She picks up the next piece of dough from the aluminium *saani*, rolls it between her palms, sprinkles dry flour onto it, drops it onto her *patli*, and starts to roll it with her *velan*. She sweeps her drooping *saree* back onto her shoulder as she turns over the *roti* on the griddle, then continues to roll the next one. She swiftly flicks the first off the griddle and onto a plate as she picks up the next one from the *patli* and drops it on the griddle. It is all one rhythmic flow.

Oh yes, I forgot to say our after-school snack is also a rolled-up *roti* smeared with ghee and sugar.

To me, one of life's biggest pleasures is the heavenly aroma of freshly cooking *rotis*. For us, it is as sacred as Baa's love that she enfolds in her cooking and in her being. Baa and Baapuji's world is filled with love, love, and love. I truly cannot recall a time when I did not feel this love from my parents or my siblings. It is just there, not said, not expressed in any fancy words, not bought with materials things, just there. Maybe I feel it because I cannot recall ever feeling judged or criticised for anything by my parents and any of my family as I am growing up. Maybe also because I feel I can just be who I am. Just who I am. Maybe.

I am happy here amidst the love and aroma of *rotis* – I feel at home.

When Baa has time, she makes savoury snacks as a weekend treat with the same love and devotion with which she makes *rotis*: *gathiya* made from chick pea flour, and *chevdo*, our favourite, made from fried moong beans, fried split chickpeas, fine potato crisps, and puffed rice spiced up with turmeric, salt, sugar and chilli powder. It takes her the whole of an afternoon to make a tin of *chevdo* even with us kids helping her. She saves a large portion in an airtight aluminium tin and sends some to the neighbouring children.

But growing up in my beloved Thika is not just about hibiscus shrubs, turiya *Panchika*, being a nuisance to my older siblings, *Aarti* at the *Mandir*, stolen mangoes, steaming spicy *mogo*, reading well in English, singing and dancing with Niru and Sima, or Baa's heavenly *rotis* rolled in her divine love. It is also a history in the making.

CHAPTER 3

HISTORY IN THE MAKING

THIKA, KENYA, 1963

I am eight years old and my first memory of being part of a significant day in history starts with Mrs. Nyame. My younger brother and I wander off to the front of the yard where Kuende and Wanjiku, our African neighbours, live. Kuende's mum is making 'ugali'. Mrs. Nyame tells me it takes a lot of practice to boil this dough without burning it. Ugali is usually eaten with meat, but as we are vegetarians, she serves us 'sukuma wiki'. My brother and I try to eat it in the traditional way, which is to pinch off a piece of the ugali dough with the right hand and shape it into a scoop by pressing into it with the thumb. I haven't quite mastered the way Kuende uses his right hand to make a scoop, picks up a bite of sukuma wiki into it, and pops it into his mouth without dropping it. We all have a few chuckles before I manage a few mouthfuls together. Mrs. Nyame says we must come back for more ugali and '*irio*' the day after tomorrow, the twelfth of December. She says this is a very special day. The date skips my little brain, but I cannot forget the irio – my favourite! I blabber excitedly about the forthcoming goodie as we walk back home.

12TH DECEMBER 1963

Everything is the same as any other day, yet something is different – a different vibe and pace to the morning. Baa and Baapuji are up early and siblings are rushing through their morning routine even though there is no school. Little brother is banging the bathroom door with one hand while pressing his crotch with the other, shouting for Bhai to come out of the bathroom. He is desperate to get in there, but Bhai is taking his time, as usual. My older sister is crying as Baa is struggling to untangle her long waist-length hair with a big brown comb. Baapuji is shaving on the veranda in front of a one-foot-by-one-foot mirror fastened to the wall with a single nail.

'Baa, why is there no school today?' I want to know.

'Because it is "*Jamhuri*" day,' she responds while plaiting my sister's long curly hair and reaching out for the white ribbons to secure the ends.

'Jam...hu... What is that?'

My brother tries to explain to me over the steaming *chai* and *roti* breakfast, but most of it is lost to my naive eight-year-old brain.

Without any warning, the sound of drums and singing breezes in from the street. We all race out through the yard, past Kuende and Wanjiku's house. They are there too, dressed in traditional Kenyan clothes today: *kitenge* and *kikoys*.

'It's Jamhuri day today!' they both shriek in excitement together.

At the gate by the main road we ogle the parade going past. Women with painted faces, feathers in their hair, beaded necklaces, and brightly coloured garments are performing '*Goma*', a local dance. Men in *kitenges,* and men draped in orange and red cloth holding spears, do another variation of *Goma*. A row of drummers leads the parade.

Mrs. Nyame is wearing feathers in her hair and is dressed in a bright *kitenge* dress as well. She hands us flags coloured in green, black and red to wave in rhythm to the singing, drumming and dancing. We join in with the singing with whatever words we can catch and get in step to the *Goma* with Kuende and Wanjiku. '*Harambe tumuse pamoja...utinde...serekari.*'

It is as if we have been transposed into another world, having not seen such celebrations and influx of people before. At midday, the dancing stops for a while. Everybody stands solemnly to sing a different song I have never heard before. I thoroughly enjoy the day eating *ugali* and *irio* with Kuende and Wanjiku, not understanding what I am celebrating.

***

Fifteen months later, in History class in school, I am able to make sense of that day. By this time, I am well versed with what was once an unfamiliar and new tune – I can sing the Kenyan national anthem by heart on my own. We all stand up in assembly to join in with the chorus every day in school.

'Ee Mungu nguvu yetu
Ilete baraka kwetu
Haki iwe ngao na mlinzi
Natukae na undugu
Amani na uhuru
Raha tupate na ustawi

'Justice be our shield and defender
May we dwell in unity
Peace and liberty
Plenty be found within our borders.

'Amkeni ndugu zetu
Tufanye sote bidii
Nasi tujitoe kwa nguvu
Nchi yetu ya Kenya
Tunayoipenda
Tuwe tayari kuilinda

'Let one and all arise
With hearts both strong and true
Service be our earnest endeavour
And our homeland of Kenya

Heritage of splendour
Firm may we stand to
defend.

'Natujenge taifa letu   'Let all with one accord
Ee, ndio wajibu wetu   In common bond united
Kenya istahili heshima   Build this our nation
Tuungane mikono   together
Pamoja kazini   And the glory of Kenya
Kila siku tuwe na shukrani.   The fruit of our labour
'O God of all creation   Fill every heart with
Bless this our land and   thanksgiving.'
nation'

My history teacher tells us, 'The East African nation, the Republic of Kenya, celebrates Independence Day on the 12th of December every year to commemorate the day of independence from Great Britain. Independence Day in Kenya is known as *"Jamhuri"*, meaning *"a republic"* in the Swahili language. Does anyone remember this?'

We share our memories of this momentous day.

He continues, 'Kenya became part of the British Protectorate of East Africa in the year 1895, and later, the British Colony of Kenya, in 1920. In the years following, the resentment of the people grew at the non-inclusion of African-Kenyans in the political process, until 1944 when they were given a chance to play a role. Unfortunately, disputes over land and cultural traditions persisted. Does anyone know who the Mau Mau were?''

Wanjiku, sitting next to me, responds, 'Is that our people who fought the white people so they would leave Kenya?'

'Yes, the movement against colonial rule began with the Mau Mau uprisings in the 1950s. By the 1960s, African political participation had increased by leaps and bounds. Independence from British rule was granted on 12th December, 1963. *Jamhuri* is a day of phenomenal historical significance for the Kenyans. Does anyone know what happened for the celebrations on 12th December?'

Most of us had heard them over the radio.

'The day began with a speech from our president, Jomo Kenyatta, at the Nyayo Stadium in Nairobi, the capital of Kenya. The defence forces and all the government dignitaries attended the event. Our Kenyan flag adorned homes and office buildings –'

'I have three flags at home, and my father bought me a new *kitenge* to wear on the day.'

A boy at the front adds, 'My uncle and aunt came over from Mombasa to celebrate with us.'

'Did anyone else have a party on the Twelfth?' the teacher asks.

The lesson ends with festive blabber.

I discover many things that day that British people learn little, if anything, about. At the age of nine, my knowledge of the British Empire and its colonies is greater than most people's living in Britain. I say this because of my conversations with someone in another part of the world over thirty years later.

CHAPTER 4

EXTENDED LOVE

THIKA, KENYA, 1964

At the age of nine, my world is not just Baa, Baapuji, siblings, school, temple and the square of green grass outside our house. It goes beyond that, to *Motabaa*.

I was the second daughter born to my parents. My Motabaa has one son and she stakes a claim to me as her adopted daughter when I am born. Motabaa is round and cuddly where Baa is sleek and slender. She ties her hair in a knot just like Baa, but her hair is fine and silky.

I do not understand all of what she says to me as a young child, but she tells me she felt an instant connection to me and had to have me as a big part of her life. Little did I know at that time that she would feel part of my soul forever; that I would think of her at sad and happy times for the rest of my life, and that she would guide and comfort me in my dreams; that she would be amongst one of the most significant people in my life, one who would bless me with the profound experience of human connections.

This extraordinary relationship extended my world to the other side, to the upper-class area of Section Nine where the affluent business people and professionals resided and where Motabaa and *Motabapuji* live. They had a house initially, and then a flat after Motabapuji retired from the post office. Baapuji and Motabapuji are peas from the same peapod – tall, handsome, with small sparkling eyes – but Motabapuji is educated and had a high-profile job, whereas Baapuji is a foreman in a Japanese-owned textile factory. Had it not been for Motabaa and Motabapuji, my world would have been confined to what was affordable within the means of Baapuji's salary. This juxtaposition of my modest and their affluent life, weekdays with my parents and siblings and weekends and holidays with Motabaa and Motabapuji, shaped my existence immeasurably on a physical, mental, and spiritual level.

Unlike Baa and Baapuji, Motabaa and Motabapuji show their love for me by taking me on outings and buying me gifts, though they do also cook me the foods I love. It is Saturday today, so, like most Saturdays, they both pick me up to spend the weekend with them. Motabapuji drives a sleek black Chevrolet and today he drives me and Motabaa to Nairobi, twenty-six miles away, for a day out. The day goes past in a flash, shopping and having dinner in a restaurant. I fall asleep on the way back and wake up the next morning in my own room with plush furniture and designer bed sheets. I hear Motabaa pottering about the flat and I recall their detached house with the papaya tree in the garden that surrounded the house, before Motabapuji's retirement and my cousin's departure to the United Kingdom.

We have tea and toast for breakfast, after which Motabaa will prepare Sunday lunch. Motabaa's routine is all very orderly and unruffled compared to the chaos of Baa's trying to fend for her large family with limited resources. Motabaa asks me what I would like for lunch.

'Can we have *garam garam bhajiya*, please?' Baa only makes this when we have guests.

'But we had that on Thursday...' she starts to say, before Motabapuji interrupts her.

'If you fancy *bhajiya*, then that is what it will be. I will run up to the grocer's and get the chickpea flour.'

That happens often. When I ask for something that Motabaa is not keen on, Motabapuji insists she make it because that is what I want.

Over Sunday lunch, we plan the following weekend together. There is a new film released which is causing a stir in the Indian film world and Motabaa says we will go to Nairobi again to see it. The movie has not been released yet at the drive-in cinema, but the indoor Shan Cinema in the Nyagara area is showing it.

By Sunday afternoon the novelty of being a spoilt only child is wearing off and I am beginning to miss the companionship of my siblings, the unarticulated pull to my parents, and the bed I share with my sister with its clean but fading homemade quilt and bedsheets. I am returned home with a gift tucked under my arm as usual.

'Motabaa got me this frock!' I show it off to everyone, but soon forget about it amidst the elation of homecoming.

Baa carefully folds the dress and puts it in the drawer that constitutes 'my wardrobe'. My wardrobe in Baa's house consists of five home-sewn cotton dresses. The pink and sage ones are hand-me-downs from my sister. Baa's friend sewed the white one with a red border, and the new purple one in a shiny fabric, Motabaa has had made for me. I also have a *kitenge*, yellow, with a triangular pattern on the bodice. I wonder if two school uniforms count as part of 'my wardrobe'?

***

I wear the pink dress to welcome my *Fai* and cousins during part of the six-week mid-year school holiday. Baa and Fai are more like sisters than sisters-in-law. They grew up together in India. Fai and my cousins get on the bus clutching their satchels for the twenty-six-mile ride from Nairobi. The bus stops at Juju, Ruiru and few other villages on the way. They walk through the market area adjoining the Thika bus stop, cross the main road, past the only restaurant and cinema in town, and across the roundabout that leads them to my grass square. Fai greets us with the same outpouring of love that she has for Bapuji and Baa. My cousins are thrilled to see us.

'How was your journey? You must be famished after that long trip. Come into the kitchen. I am just about to make *rotis*,' Baa says as she extends an affectionate hug to each in turn.

'I will roll them.' Fai snatches the *velan* from Baa's hand, tucks her indigo-coloured *saree* under her legs, and slides herself onto the *patla* next to the *saqdi*. She matches her speed to Baa's, rolling the *rotis* while Baa forms the balls of dough. As the *rotis* make their way to the pile, the house is filled by a scrumptious fragrance. There is an added magic in the air today – the *rotis*, curry, and companionship are evocative of the divinity of family.

The week speeds past us. We visit the nearby waterfalls, temple, and Uhuru Park. We play cards and read books. There is swapping of comics and Roald Dahl, Enid Blyton and James Hadley Chase books, between cousins. Fai tells us stories about the family she adores.

She tells us my grandfather settled in Tanzania, (then called Tanganyika), also a British colony, in the early 1900s, where his first child, my Motabapuji, was born and began his education. Later, my grandfather travelled back to India for a holiday, accompanied by his young daughter and his wife. My Grandmother was expecting Baapuji at the time and Fai tells us that he was born in Porbandar, in Gujarat, in an area called Chhaya Plot. My grandfather was also born in Porbandar, which is the birthplace of Mahatma Gandhi, the most well-known Gujerati in the world and in the history books.

Unfortunately, there was a tragic turn in the family's life while they were back in India. My grandfather contracted a sudden illness and passed away. His dream of educating all his children was shattered. Instead of going to school, my father and Fai had to work to help my grandmother run the house. They also did not have the means to return to Tanzania. My grandfather had left my Motabapapuji in Tanzania with his older sister and this is why Motabapapuji was better educated than the rest of his siblings.

My father, when he grew to be of an eligible age, had an arranged marriage with my mother who was from a village called Daiyar, not far from Porbandar. Back in Tanzania, my Motabapapuji was working for The British Post Office. After several assignments, he was transferred to Thika and my father, mother and Fai were able to join him there. Fai tells us about the gruelling ocean journey from India to Kenya lasting weeks in a *dhow*. Fai got married and settled in Nairobi while my father got a job and settled near Motabapuji. I gathered later that Baapuji wanted to study but did not have the means to.

Fai's stories feel surreal, too far-fetched to be true in our little innocent worlds. But, yet, huddled around Fai with my siblings and cousins, ears tweaked to her every word, I feel safe and happy to my core.

CHAPTER 5

THE THREE WATERFALLS

THIKA, KENYA, 1965 - 1968

Talking about our little innocent worlds takes me back to the ten-mile-radius world of my ten-year-old self. I try to imagine ten miles stretching beyond the one mile of home, school and the grass square surrounded by a gutter next to my house. What is beyond this...?

I am walking home for lunch on a school day as usual, panting, trying to keep up with my brother who, for some unknown reason, is not affected by the scorching sun and plumes of red soil that strike my brown plastic shoes with each hurried step. I can see the end of the parting in his head of dark hair, the white shirt on his back, khaki shorts down to his white socks and faded black shoes, as his satchel bobs up and down, matching his eager footsteps.

'Bhai... Bhai...' I shout after him, '*aaste chalone*, (walk slower, please)!'

It gets worse as he accelerates into a run, completely ignoring my protests at being left behind. This is not very kind to a hungry, flustered, tortured-by-the-sun, little girl with dusty, brown plastic shoes and I fume within. Then he disappears from my low-ceiling horizon completely.

Eventually, I can see home in the midst of the shadows of the trees, leaves dancing amongst the yellow of the sweltering sunshine. I see our house but I also see what looks like the back of a minibus tucked between the alley entry to our house and the fabric shop next to it. Ah... now I know why Bhai broke into a run – Baapuji is home and he has borrowed the factory minibus this lunchtime. Whenever Baapuji gets a chance to bring the minibus home at lunchtime, we know it is adventure time! The rumblings of hunger in my stomach are taken over now by rumblings of excitement. After our hasty and tasty lunch, my siblings and I, as well as the children of the surrounding neighbourhood, will be having a tour beyond our one-mile radius world.

'Shall we have a ride to the waterfall today?' he calls out to the group of children that have gathered around the minibus after lunch. '*Chalto, Chalto* (Come on, Come on),' he gestures, inviting his eager audience.

'Yeah...Ha...' we all yell in unison and excitedly pile into our seats.

Baapuji makes a right turn at the end of the road, driving past the *Gurduwara*, and then takes a left. We peer out with wonder at the green pastures planted with maize and pineapple as Baapuji heads onwards. We drive past a row of houses, some are made of stone and some of corrugated iron, with allotments next to them... Jerome lives in one of them. As we pass his house, we can see him tending his vegetables. Baapuji slows as we cheer to draw Jerome's attention and Jerome waves to us.

Soon, we are waiting in anticipation for the sharp bend bearing to the right. As Baapuji skilfully takes the turn, we all gasp ecstatically at the sight and sound of the rush of the waterfall beyond the bridge. But then Baapuji says we will have to turn back from the bridge so we are not late for the afternoon session of school! We all howl with objection, even though we know that Baapuji is a man of principle and discipline and there is no way we are going to be late returning to school. We head back, but the waterfall story does not end here.

***

I am thirteen years old now and feeling good in my white dress with its red border that falls just above my knees, as opposed to half-way down my calf when I was first given it. Motabaa says this white dress makes me look like a fairy. It's a December Saturday, which means no school, and Motabaa and Motabapuji are on holiday in India, so it is a day for more waterfall adventures.

Thika is surrounded by three waterfalls: Chania Falls, Thika Falls, and Fourteen Falls. A group of us, including two of my siblings, decide to walk up to Chania Falls, which is the nearest and easiest to get to. We tell our parents our plans for the day and set off on our journey. We chat as we walk past the temple and call out to Ritu who lives in the house a few yards beyond. She decides to join us. At the end of the road, we take a shortcut onto Falls Road. The equator sun flashes on the windscreen of the odd car that whizzes up the narrow road lined by maize and pineapple plantations. The sunlit landscape in-between is splashes of brown and green.

Half an hour later we get to the row of houses where Jerome lives, but today he is nowhere in sight. Saturday is his day to sell his vegetables in the only grocery supermarket in our small town. We walk past Kariuki's house. Kariuki comes to see Baa when he can find no work as a labourer. Usually Baa does all the housework herself, but she likes to help out Karuiki when he is struggling to feed his family. He does the *fagiyo* (sweeping) and *fanguza* (mopping), and in return she feeds him a big pile of *rotis*, packs some for his children, and gives him a few shillings on top; often, she will give him Baapuji's old shirts too.

31

'*Jambo, habari gani*? (Hello, how are you?)' he greets us as we walk past.

'*Mzuri sana*, (Very well),' we reply. '*Tutaonana*, (See you later).' We wave and carry on.

We are now walking downhill, which is an indication that the Falls is not far off. As we approach the bend, we see and hear the waterfall. We run up to the bridge from where we can see the water gushing down into the valley basin. On the right, a five-minute walk beyond the bridge, is the Blue Post Hotel. The only way down to the valley is through the hotel's gardens and then a steep climb down the slippery, rugged, rocky stairway.

We scurry in a race to get to the bottom of the valley. I follow my sister who holds my hand to help me down the slippery stairway. As we descend, we are cooled by splashes of water from the falls as it hits the rocks below. I see my Bhai sitting on one of these with his feet in the water and soon join him. We chat excitedly as we splatter each other with water. Then we have a game of pebble-throwing. I feel at home here too, I am happy.

Even though I am half-soaked, I want to follow Bhai along the rocks under the bridge to the other side of the Chania River, but my sister persuades me not to – the climb back to the hotel will be exhausting. And it is. We slump on the benches in the hotel garden to get our breath back. We use the toilets and then sit in the garden watching the guests as they enjoy their meals and drinks on the patio. Bhai gets us some squash and popcorn, which we relish.

We set off for home, aiming to get there before dusk otherwise Baa and Baapuji will get worried. I am dried off by the time we reach the house, but my sister gets a telling off from Baa because her clothes are all muddied and still damp.

'You will catch a cold,' Baa frets. 'I shall make some *kadhi* with lots of ginger to warm you up. The ginger will wave off the chill in your body.'

I am exhausted but I help Baa to knead the *roti* dough for supper.

***

A few months later, we visit Thika Falls. This is further away so we have to rely on Baapuji borrowing the factory minibus or on visitors with a car. Baapuji and his Japanese boss have made a plan to get their children together to play and have a day out so we set off after lunch on a Saturday. Joining us are a few neighbourhood children for whom the curiosity of meeting Japanese children has made them abandon their plan of playing *Gili Danda*.

Baapuji takes the usual route up to the bridge. On school-day outings to the falls, this is where he turns back, but today we continue across to the other side. On the left is the road to Nairobi. To the right, we see Chania Falls gushing down into the valley beneath the gardens of the Blue Post Hotel. Baapuji carries on along this road for half a mile and turns into a carpark on the left. We all shuffle out and run over to the railing from where Thika Falls greets us with gusto. We are taking in the mesmerizing sounds of the gushing water when a big expensive-looking car pulls up into the car park.

We are in awe of this magnificent-looking vehicle from which a short oriental-looking man and two children emerge. Baapuji's boss introduces his children, telling us their ages are nine and twelve. He smiles and tells us that after the visit to Fourteen Falls we can all go to the Blue Post Hotel for some refreshments. The Japanese children join us in the minibus. They cannot speak Swahili or Gujerati and their broken English and accent are difficult to understand. They are also shy so not much conversation happens with them on the ten-minute journey to Fourteen Falls. Our animated conversations continue to flow, with them listening on with inquisitive expressions.

We disembark in the small clearing before Fourteen Falls and take in the breath-taking scene. Against the backdrop of hills and trees, fourteen streams of water arc, all parted by a foot or so but connected in the same forceful race to hit the thirsty rocks of the riverbed below. I often savour these magnificent sights in my dreams.

Later, we drive back to the hotel and take our seats in the garden under the thatched sun-shade. First, we have cool Coca-Cola from the bottle with a straw. Next, the waiter brings a large tray with rows of bowls containing three yellow-coloured slices each in a thick, syrupy solution. The food in the bowls looks like smooth orange segments at closer glance, but these are not like the fresh oranges that Baa buys from Jerome. We are each given a bowl and spoon. We take a few bites of the smooth, sweet fruit, puzzled by what it might be. We do not understand the Japanese boss's accent when he tells us this is 'peach' we are eating. It is only many years later, in a faraway land, that I discover this was tinned peaches. Being brought up on fresh organic food from Jerome and his friends' allotments made tinned food an exotic experience for all of us.

***

I have passed my secondary education with a distinction and it is time for me to join my older siblings in England to further my education. My beloved Thika and its remarkable natural surroundings, the innocence of childhood years, fade away into oblivion for many years until these sweet poignant memories are reignited some thirty years later.

CHAPTER 6

ENGLAND, HOME FROM HOME

ENGLAND, SEPTEMBER, 1971

I am sixteen years old now. It's a crisp September day under a grey sky as I leave Heathrow airport with Bhai who has made the trip from Birmingham to meet me. I have no idea what I expect England to be like, as I had only a handful of photos to go by that Bhai and my sister had sent me. They came to England in 1968. The British government has imposed entry visas for Asians coming to England from Kenya, so even though Baapuji has a British passport, there is a delay in the rest of the family joining us. They will follow a few years after me.

We get a coach from the airport, and as I write this I try to recall that journey and any shocks and surprises that I experienced. I slept for most of it but I remember Bhai holding forth about the advertising on all the huge billboards we passed. I notice when I come out of my slumber that there are no dusty brown roads. I am used to narrow tarmac ones, but here I am on a massive road with cars and lorries speeding away in three lanes. The landscape on either side is a lush deep green. I think of the green and brown sunlit land I have left behind. We are closing in on a built-up area. I can see red brick buildings with tiled roofs and my eyes have difficulty taking in the rows and rows of these buildings joined to each other. I step into one of these red buildings, a three-bed terraced house, and take in how enclosed it all feels compared to the openness of the yard and veranda of my home in Thika.

Settling in is relatively smooth-going as Bhai, my sister, and my cousins guide me through the British way of life. I do not recall feeling homesick because I have my siblings, and my Fai and cousins live across the road. I think of Baa and Baapuji often, but I soon get engrossed in my studies at college, doing my A-Levels in Social Sciences. Apart from the size of Birmingham and the many European people in my surroundings, it feels like home from home. I am used to the English language, having been taught the same curriculum in Kenya as is taught in schools in Britain. I can speak Gujerati with my family, and there is ample Indian vegetarian food available in local shops.

Fai tells me this was not always the case. She and her family came to Britain in the early sixties. She tells me about the harsh winter conditions without central heating and relying on kerosene heaters for warmth. Some houses did not have bathrooms and they had to go to the public baths once a week to bathe and wash their hair. There was a lack of Indian ingredients and other goods in the shops. What little was available was bought from door-to-door salesmen touting a variety of spices, lentils, flours, *sarees* and so on. Some of these salesmen are multimillionaires now, having started from these humble beginnings and the safety-net of a supportive family network. My older siblings, who came three years before me, shared some of these challenges but worked hard and bought a family home. I find all this hard to take in, having walked into a comfortable, warm and welcoming, centrally-heated house with a bathroom on my first day in England.

Three weeks after arriving in Birmingham, I go to my first social spiritual event. We are gathered in a hired venue because there is no community hall adjoining our temple like we have in Thika. As I walk in, the same incense of sandalwood soothes my nostrils. There is no altar for the deities, but instead a makeshift shrine adorned with daisies. However, the female deity has the same bright attire, reassuring smile, and twinkle in her eye. The bells chime for the *Aarti* Ritual and the hymn is sung by everyone with zeal. At the end of the ritual, the *Maharaj* turns around and circles the lamp towards all the devotees. An inner peace and sense of belonging creeps into my being. I wonder if I am *really* in England because here again I feel at home and I am happy.

Languages, food, family, home, connectedness, belonging, education – they are all here. But there is one thing that I have here that I did not in Thika: a thick winter coat. Bhai buys me a pair of gloves and a hat to go with my beige hand-me-down coat. 'Put these on,' he says. 'We will go into town to see the Christmas lights and have *garam garam* chips for lunch.'

At college, I do not realise I have to take off my coat once I get to class, having never owned or needed a coat before. '*Is she, or is she not, going to wear her coat all through class?*' Unbeknownst to me, my fellow students are placing bets, until a kind student points me in the right direction, towards the cloakroom.

Another memory that stands out is that I cannot understand a word my lecturer says in his broad Glaswegian accent even though I have a good command of English. After more years in the United Kingdom, I come to love the Scottish accent; and the stunning scenic beauty of Scotland even more. '*It is mostly raining and very cold in Scotland,*' I hear people around me say, but I did not have to go to Scotland for that – my first winter in England gives me plenty.

Yet the warmth of the people around me has diffused any concerns I may have had about the dark, cold English winters. The warmth of my family, and sprinkles of chilli powder! Chilli has heat-inducing properties and balances the cold in the body. By the time my parents and younger siblings have joined us, I have acquired a taste for chips with tinned baked beans and macaroni cheese, (also from a tin), with a sprinkle of chilli.

***

With Baa and Baapuji now here, our happy family times together with Fai and my cousins are restored. After a week of work or study, we all look forward to enjoying the weekend with each other. The men do the shopping and odd jobs around the house on Saturday. Baa and the girls cook the traditional Sunday dinner: *pappadoms*, a savoury item like *bhajiya* or *samosas*, vegetable curry, rice and lentil soup, and a sweet dish made from milk and vermicelli. The younger generation now calls this 'DBS' – *Daal* (lentil), *Bhaat* (rice), and *Shak* (curry). We are all grown up now and have bigger appetites, so the pile of *rotis* is almost a foot high. My sister and I start on it at noon and just about finish it for one-thirty when lunch is served. After clearing up, we all gather in the living room for the Sunday matinee which is typically a western starring John Wayne. Cups of Indian tea do the rounds halfway through the movie, followed by a light supper of leftovers, and then it's Monday again.

There is a little family time on weekdays too. I am in my bedroom working on my college assignment when I hear Bhai's voice from the hallway,

'Everyone, come down! "Mind Your Language" is on in five minutes.'

The assignment can wait. I clamber down the stairs, not wanting to miss sitting in my favourite spot by the fire in the living room, but I am too late – my sister has got there first. I try to squeeze in but she pushes me away.

'*Per favore.*' My younger brother walks in, imitating the Italian character in the sitcom. We join in, going over dialogue from previous episodes amid bouts of hilarity.

This joy of being together, my and Fai's families, is alive to this day; DVDs and YouTube are great inventions that keep these poignant memories alive. But I miss Motabaa and Motabapuji who have moved to India, although their son, my cousin, lives twenty miles away. Sadly, they both pass away within a short time of each other and never get the opportunity to visit their family in England. My cousin and I are supported by the family and, although life goes on as usual, I will feel Motabaa's presence in my dreams and around me during significant moments in my life.

I pass my A-Levels and Bhai wants me to go to university, but I meet my future husband at the local youth club where I like to sing and I fall in love and get married.

BIRMINGHAM, ENGLAND, 1979

At twenty-four, my inherent needs are buried amidst the events of the next few years because my son is born. It is one of the happiest days of my life. Happiness, and shock! My memories of being raised as a child do not serve me well in coping with this tiny little human being screaming in his cot. My husband is at work and I am alone in the house and I do not know what to do. As the first grandchild born in the family, and in England, I have no model to follow. The health visitors are there for support but little of what they suggest seems to help.

There are terry nappies to wash and dry, which is quite a chore on a two-degree winter day. There are bottles of puréed food, packages of dried food, painkillers, vitamin drops, a bottle sterilizer, cot, pushchair, stair-gate, baby grows, towels, bath-chair – baby this and baby that – none of which were around when I was little. All my siblings and I grew up in a homemade *ghodiyu,* (cot), nappies made from old garments, and food for the family which

Baa puréed for the little ones. Bath-time took place in a plastic basin. That was all.

Bringing up a boisterous baby, a tempestuous toddler, and then a cheeky child, my journey as a new mother is like climbing Mount Kenya without doing the fitness training first – I am panting and stopping for breath most of the time. Often I am in pain as I struggle to get to the top, but along the journey, the magnificent joyful discoveries, the ecstasy when I reach the next landmark, and the view when I get to the top, are an accolade gifted from God in person.

My daughter is born three years later. As with my son, it is love at first sight. I hold her in my arms a few minutes after being born and never want to put her down. She is another kindred spirit joining me on my life's journey. With her it is like revisiting all the remarkable memories of the climb to Mount Kenya, only not so challenging as she is of a gentler character than my son.

She is three years old now and sitting in her baby chair in the kitchen. I am making *rotis* for dinner, not seated on the floor on a *patla* like Baa in the open kitchen in Thika, but standing up and rolling them out on the kitchen worktop. I keep my daughter amused with her toy *patli* and *velan* by passing her a little ball of dough so she can play at making *rotis*. This is the first skill that Indian girls are taught when they learn to cook. How we make *rotis* – the way we pick up, shape and handle the balls of dough before rolling, how we hold the *velan,* and the movement and swirl of our arms as we roll out – says a lot about our personality.

An English friend comes to dinner. She is amazed by the *roti* rolling technique which is taken for granted in Indian women's way of life. I invite her to have a go at rolling one. She makes several attempts and we end up with a small pile of *rotis*, one that is a square shape, one the shape of India, and other shapes that do not have a recognizable description but lead to fits of laughter. She vows to add this to her bucket-list, aiming to produce a pile of *rotis* as round and precise as mine. This is a worthy addition to any bucket-list, to learn to roll out and cook *rotis* as smoothly and effortlessly as Baa did with mesmerizing rhythm and love. Suddenly, the *roti* saga is interrupted,

'Look mum, I'm Superman!'

My six-year-old son in his Superman outfit is standing on the dining table, ready to 'fly' to the floor. I run up and grab him before he attempts the stunt he saw on television earlier. This is not the first time he has tried to emulate his heroes. He is a close second to Dennis the Menace on his exuberant days, but quite the Popeye when helping his mum, dad and little sister after pretending he's eaten all his spinach!

The children's antics are confined to the house as there is no green grass square for them to play freely in. In our multi-cultural neighbourhood, my children's play-time with other children is confined to small gardens. A mother in England would contact the police if her child disappeared for the whole day, whereabouts unknown. In Thika, our parents knew we would be home for supper even though they rarely had eyes on us.

There is no equator sun here. Not that I miss it. I occasionally think about it in the peak of winter and the short, dark days, but the bright lights of Christmas and the festive ambience warm our hearts and weave stories that my children will pass on to their children. We did not have the tremendous pleasure of walking in the snow in the park with our parents and the fun of snow fights either!

BIRMINGHAM, ENGLAND, 1987

At the age of thirty-two, I am juggling two boisterous children with a job in customer services and the addition of my husband's family. Even though in my birth family there were no restrictions upon my spirit and sense of self, tradition expects that I, the daughter-in-law, make my husband's family my own and assume responsibility for their welfare. I take this duty seriously, and my parents and siblings are supportive, but it takes me further away from myself. My siblings-in-law help me with childcare in return for the effort I make towards securing their futures, but all is not hunky dory. Life never is, so I try not to judge those challenges and carry on. Eventually, they are all married and settled in their own homes. My upbringing has taught me to love them unconditionally, so they remain an integral part of our life to-date.

CHAPTER 7

INDIA, ANCESTRAL HOME

I am thirty-five now and have lived in England for nineteen years. It is January 1990, and we are off on our first lifetime family holiday to India.

It is literally the sweetest assault on all our senses and the culture shock takes days to wear off. It is nothing at all like my introduction to Britain. After the freezing temperatures of the English winter, stepping off the plane and being hit by the dry heat with its distinct musky smell still lingers in my psyche. Travelling in a taxi from the airport to the hotel and being taken aback by the sea of only brown faces after thirty-five years of living amongst multicultural faces is the most striking aspect of that initial entry to the country of my ancestors.

'I thought England would be a shock to the system when I first arrived but actually India has completely bomb-shelled me,' I say to my family, and they agree wholeheartedly.

It takes a few weeks to get used to India.

I will not go on about *rotis* here, although this is where they originate, and instead tell you that one of the first notable differences in cultural behaviour is how Indians go to the cinema. You could not have experienced India without experiencing Indian cinema, the largest film industry in the world.

I am near a cinema in Porbandar with my husband and children, aged eight and eleven, as well as a relative who has been escorting us since our arrival, and I am trying to fathom the chaos outside the cinema hall. In the crowd, there are young men eyeing up the pretty girls, dressed in jeans and some in traditional *salwar kameez*, the men, flirting and whistling whenever an opportunity arises. There are many families with young children clutching the hands of their dads and mums. There are men in turbans, and men without turbans. There are Hindu women in bright *sarees* with *bindis* on their foreheads, and Muslim women in *burkhas* closely following their male relatives. There are older couples and older single men not wanting to miss out on seeing the latest offering from the big Indian film star, Amitabh Bachchan, and there are babies crying in their mother's arms while their fathers negotiate the box office.

In the absence of any queuing system or order prior to entering the cinema hall, everyone is trying to manoeuvre forward in the confusion and crowd. And once inside, the noise and chatter is akin to a busy café in a railway station. I catch the bemused look on my son's and daughter's faces as they too try to make sense of the chaos. My son asks me why the lady had not left her baby with a baby-sitter. Our relative chuckles and says there is no need as babies are welcome in a cinema even though they may cry through the film. I think about this scenario in an English cinema, which makes me cringe with embarrassment. Then, suddenly, there is silence and everyone stands to sing the Indian national anthem before the film starts.

Jana-gana-mana-adhinayaka jaye he
Bharata-bhagya-vidhata
Punjaba-Sindhu-Gujarata-Maratha
Dravida-Utkala-Banga,
Vindhya-Himachala-Yamuna-Ganga,
uchchala-jaladhi-taranga
Tava shubha name jage, tava shubha asisa
mage,
gahe tava jaya-gatha.
Jana-gana-mangala-dayaka jaya he
Bharata-bhagya-vidhata.
Jaya he, Jaya he, Jaya he,
jaya jaya jaya, jaya he!

Thou art the ruler of the minds of all
people,
Dispenser of India's destiny.
Thy name rouses the hearts of the Punjab,
Sind, Gujarat, and Maratha,
Of the Dravid and Orissa and Bengal;
it echoes in the hills of the Vindhya and
Himalaya, mingles in the music of the
Jamuna and the Ganges, and is chanted by
the waves of the Indian sea.
They pray for thy blessings and sing thy praise.
The saving of all people waits in thy hand,
Thou dispenser of India's destiny.
Victory, victory, victory to thee.

I half know the lyrics to this and my children look on in bemusement
at the fervour with which it is sung by the crowd. I wonder if this
would be possible in cinema halls in Birmingham.

In Britain and Kenya, I am used to silence during the film and polite behaviour towards fellow cinema-goers, and to some extent these are evident here in India too. However, what is most striking is the audience's verbal interaction with the characters on the screen. The shouting out of comments; the clapping and singing along with songs; the *'Wah Wah'* (expression of appreciation), cheers and boos at the highs and lows in the plot. Needless to say, we all join in the singing and clapping in an effort to be *'desi'*, (authentic Indian), and *'freshy'*, a term coined by third-generation Indians in England.

All through the film, as the audience shouts at the screen, telling Amitabh Bachchan he looks dashing in his blue embroidered *Shervani* shirt or cheering and clapping when he fights off the villain and gets the girl, I am thinking of the reaction of an English audience. Maybe there is a point in letting go of some of our inhibitions and really living the emotions of the characters on the screen. One may recoil in horror at the thought, but I say this because the feeling of exhilaration and excitement as we all streamed out of the cinema hall is permanently etched as one of my finest Indian holiday memories.

We step out of the cinema and into another extraordinary experience. We have been here for two weeks now but still cannot get over how the roads work in India. There are cars on the road, of course, but also cows, rickshaws, carts, lorries, people of all ages – all sorts. We watch in amazement at how the people cross the roads despite all this chaos, and how the rickshaws manoeuvre through tight, miniscule gaps in the traffic to get us to our destinations. I have seen some of this in Bollywood movies but, even then, seeing it on film and actually being here in person in the midst of it all is 'a different kettle of fish', as the British saying goes. And if it is so for me, then imagine what it is like for my children who have not been exposed to Indian culture as much as I have.

Shopping is another such bomb-shell experience. In Britain, I buy clothes at a fixed price. I pick out what I like from a rack, go to the check-out, pay, and it can all be done in a few minutes. But not so here. Here, we go into a *saree* shop. A *saree* is a length of cloth six yards long, of various types and designs of fabric. There are many regional variations in how it is worn, but it is typically wrapped around the body lengthways, once, from the midriff, over a matching petticoat, then half of it is pleated to the front and the rest is passed under one shoulder and pinned over the other, over a short blouse. You cannot visit India and not come back with a bag full of *sarees*; at least, not in our family.

The assistant greets us, invites us to sit down. Seats are strategically placed by the merchandise. He asks us if we would like a drink, '*Kuchh thanda ya garam*, (Do you prefer a hot drink or cold drink)?' Then he goes on to show us a range of *sarees* in several styles. He even wraps a few around himself so we can see the full impact when it is worn.

'Mum, he can drape a saree quicker than I can,' my daughter remarks when she sees the speed at which he pleats, tucks, and flings the end of the garment over his shoulder.

Our heads are buzzing. We have seen umpteen sarees, and the more we see, the more perplexed we get. My son walks out of the shop. He cannot take this 'women's stuff' any more.

'Wait until you have a wife,' my daughter teases him as he makes for the door.

'I was after a silk one, but those chiffon ones are really pretty too. Do you have any the colour of this silk one in the chiffon fabric?' I ask.

The assistant disappears into the storeroom and brings out yet another pile, and so it goes on for a few more hours. In between all the viewing, we are offered more drinks and snacks.

We think it is nearly over when at last we choose three: a cerise-pink silk one, a turquoise chiffon one. and a cheaper, black, artificial silk one for less formal occasions. But I am forgetting there is no fixed price. We have probably been quoted three times the actual cost. It is apparent from our accents and the way we are dressed that we are non-residential Indians (NRIs). We were told the local people can spot the NRIs instantly just by the way we walk and gesture. Needless to say, I do not have Baa's skill of bargaining, and it is not the 'done' thing in Britain anyway, so I come across as an amateur. We end up paying twice the price a local would pay. The only consolation is that it is still cheaper than it would be at home.

By the time we set foot outside again, it is dusk and we are all exhausted. Tomorrow we are travelling to Rajkot, which has a handful of fixed-price shops. I sigh with relief at this news. On our way back to the hotel, we drive through a less popular shopping area. I spot a small shop selling utensils. By small, I mean *small*. It is amazing how the retailers in this part of the world cram their merchandise into a five-foot-by-five-foot space. Piles and piles of pots and pans.

'Please can you stop here. I would like to look at some *sufuriyas*.'

The rickshaw driver gives me a blank look and I repeat my request. He again gives me a blank look and I again I repeat my request. He stops the rickshaw and turns around to the back seat.

'*Aap kya kehe rahe ho,* (I do not understand what you are saying).'

I hear a burst of laughter from dear hubby. 'Of course he would not get it. You are saying "*sufuriya*", which is Swahili for '*pan*'. How is he going to know this?'

We all crack up with laughter.

We relate this story to an Indian couple we have befriended at our hotel. The lady says, 'I am impressed by how you speak in all three languages, all at the same time. Sometimes you do it in the same sentence.' I had not noticed this until it was pointed out to me, an example of how we can be oblivious to the obvious when absorbed in our own normality.

But those are not the only things that are exhilarating about India. The food is mind-blowing, or rather, taste-bud-blowing.

Despite my ancestors migrating across the Indian Ocean to Africa, and their off-spring then settling in Britain, the traditional Indian meal is still served a few times a week at home. We are sat around a table in a restaurant in Porbandar that is serving the traditional buffet. The food is served in a stainless-steel plate divided into ten sections. The waiters rotate between tables serving *kichadi*, *kadhi*, millet *rotlo*, *chapattis*, spinach curry, potato and *turiya* curry, *sambharo*, mixed vegetable *bhajiyas*, mint chutney and *siro*. This is one of the most satisfying meals of my life, being served the food from its place of origin after thirty-five years of waiting. I can sense Baa's love in this food and my eyes well up. The glossy buttered *chapatis* remind me of her complexion, the spices, of her vibrancy, and the *siro,* of her sweetness of nature. I feel suddenly at home. I am happy.

'Are you okay?' my dear hubby asks.

'More than okay,' I say. 'These are tears of happiness and gratitude.'

I promise myself I will endeavour to keep this tradition of love and food alive with my children and future grandchildren in England.

'Mum, will you teach me how to make this kind of *siro*,' my daughter asks as she polishes the last mouthful from her small stainless-steel bowl. Luckily, both my children have a passion for cooking so I do not envisage this to be challenging in any way.

'This *turiya* curry tastes so yummy. I suppose because it is fresh, and not the kind we get in England which is imported and preserved for transport until it gets to our shop shelves,' my son says.

'I am glad you are enjoying the food today. I don't want to be looking everywhere for chips like we did yesterday.'

'We want chips, Mum. We want chips!' my children protest after two weeks of traditional Gujerati food.

There are no fish-and-chip takeaways on every corner. We ask for them in restaurants but get none, so we have a go at making our own at the home of our distant relative. The potatoes and cooking oil are not the same, and there is no vinegar. The finger-length strips of fried potato do not capture the enticing aroma as you walk past a fish-and-chip shop in Britain, nor the experience of a *garam garam* chip melting in your mouth, especially in the glare of Christmas lights. And so the *'We want chips"* record plays until we are back at home.

CHAPTER 8

RE-INVENTING MYSELF

BIRMINGHAM UNIVERSITY, ENGLAND, 1991

I am thirty-six years old now, with a full-time job, my son starting secondary school, taking care of my in-laws, and there is not much space for me. Kenya and India fade away with the daily grind. My husband is affectionate and attentive as always, but there is something missing, something is rousing waves of discontent in my core.

I yearn for intellectual creativity and stimulation, absent in my monotonous job and domestic routines, so I enrol at university as a mature student. I do not feel a passion for maths and science subjects, so I pursue a professional qualification in social care first. The modules on psychology fascinate me. I am intrigued by human behaviours and drawn to their social and psychological aspects, so I decide to pursue a degree in Counselling Psychology. I adore university life. I love the learning environment and this feeling of strength in my psyche as each day moves on to the next. My fellow students think I am crazy when I say I love the assignments and research projects. Call me crazy, I do not care, I just love it.

I am sitting in a lecture on person-centred models and my lecturer is talking about Carl Rogers' theories on the core human conditions of acceptance, congruence, and non-judgement and how these legitimise our existence and afford recognition of our being. I learn how this kind of approval strengthens the bond between approver and approved and provides a safe psychological space for growth.

On my drive back home, and for many days after, I think about approval and I think about my parents, siblings, Motabaa and Motabapuji, and my cousins. I reflect on my fellow students in class who shared experiences of being criticized or even physically abused by their families and partners. I have no memory of being castigated or abused by anyone at home and I realise that my parents instinctively knew what we children needed in order to grow into happy, fearless and independent adults: they did not have much materially, but they showered us with approval, acceptance and unconditional love.

This was not the case in a particular relationship in primary school though. My fears and insecurities tumble out the following semester when studying Aaron Becks' cognitive behavioural theories. I am taken back to that day in primary school, defending myself before the class, and the bullying by the rich kid haunts me. I try to apply Becks' theories and put great effort into turning my negative beliefs about myself into positive ones. I challenge my belief that I am not powerful because I lived in the less well-off part of town as a child. I reframe that and begin to believe that everybody is equally important irrespective of their financial status. Just because I lived in the poor part of town does not make me a lesser human being or a person of less importance than others. This change in belief begins to improve my self-confidence, particularly in social settings.

As it turns out, I meet this rich kid from school at a Thika reunion in London later that year. He spots me from across the hotel function room and rushes towards me.

'It is so great to see you, Hansa. I often think about you. After all, you came second in our final year of primary school, and I never saw you study hard or revise much for your exams. You were always out playing with your siblings or helping your Baa with housework. You and your siblings were academically gifted, I expect you are very successful in your career now.'

He gives me a warm hug and says a lot in our conversation which affirms me as equal to him. He shows great interest in my progress in life. I can see he is not the same person who felt threatened by me in school, he has matured in his attitudes now as an adult.

Back at university, one of my assignments is about catharsis. I choose to focus on anger management and its relationship to culture, stress and wellbeing. I learn that as humans it is inevitable that we will feel angry because anger is the most basic of all emotions. My thoughts turn to what feels like the first big life challenge of my life: when I married by my own choice and moved into a family that was the complete opposite of mine.

On the second day of my married life, there was a massive aggressive outburst from my stepmother-in-law about nothing very significant. I went into shock, never having experienced anything like this. I had never heard raised voices from Baa and Baapuji. I soon learned that outbursts in my husband's family were a regular occurrence. He was supportive, so I formed the illusion that this was not affecting me. My mother's words to me on being a married woman were to look after everyone in my new family, to ignore my mother-in-law's behaviour, and to be a dutiful daughter-in-law. Her belief and conditioning were that it is virtuous to be passive and a woman earns respect in her family this way.

Back at university, I am in a personal development group, which is part of the syllabus. A group member is sharing a traumatic experience and I offer her a solution. The facilitator asks how she might be feeling, and I offer another solution. The facilitator asks again how she might be feeling, and I offer yet another solution. The facilitator says, 'Hansa, are you in touch with your feelings? This is not about solutions but about how well you can empathise with a person's emotions.'

This statement hits me like a bombshell. How might my group member be *feeling*? What was I feeling? Had I ever been in touch with my feelings?

Unbeknownst to me, this is the root cause of my burgeoning health problems: tightness in my chest and rashes on my skin. I am tested for asthma and eczema, neither of which is verified. So I begin my journey to connect emotionally, starting with myself. I keep a diary of events and associated feelings. I learn to accept anger as a valid human emotion and explore ways of expressing it safely. My journal entries after that day are rather longer than before.

For the topic of my thesis, I choose stress management. In my research, I come across literature on stress caused by repressed emotions, and the emotional overload that can ensue. This is a light-bulb moment for me. I have an overload of repressed anger and all the resulting symptoms of this stress: tightness in my chest, skin rashes, irritability, cystitis, and so on.

I am sitting in the library and in my reading somewhere it asks if the significant people in my life have given me permission to express my anger in healthy ways and modelled this to me. Another light-bulb moment! I remember what happened next like it happened yesterday. I come home to an empty house and so practice one of the anger management techniques I have read. Using not so many nice words, I give myself the permission to be angry by verbalising my feelings at an imaginary mother-in-law. I cannot describe my sense of relief!

From then on, I do not wait for anyone to give me permission to express my negative feelings, be they anger, sadness or fear. It all comes out. I write it down. I learn to use the Gestalt Empty Chair Technique wherein you imagine the person you are angry at sitting in the chair and verbalise your feelings at them. The tightness in my chest and my other symptoms begin to disappear as I work through my entire emotional overload. I tell my children now to acknowledge others' feelings as well as their own and I encourage them to express theirs in safe ways.

***

At the next Thika reunion, I meet one of my best friends from primary school. She lived in Section Nine and is kind, gentle and down to earth. She says, 'You have to sing today! Remember when you used to sing in the school playground? We all used to gather around you and ask you to sing the latest numbers on radio? Remember I sang the chorus when you performed at the school function in our final year? It's a shame the others are not here today, it would have been great to do a retake on our performance.'

'Yes, I remember,' I tell her. I also tell her that I am part of a Bollywood band with a keyboard player, drummer, *tabla* player, saxophonist, and four vocalists, including myself. We perform at all kinds of private functions, and occasionally organise our own events. I tell her we have a stage show in Birmingham Town Hall next month and she and I exchange phone numbers.

The next week, our band is performing at a wedding reception in Cardiff. The groom is Punjabi-British, and the bride is Welsh-British, so we are surprised there is only Indian food on the menu. The groom's father tells me,

'Actually, we are hosting the reception jointly, but the bride's family love Indian food and wanted only that.'

As the food is served, we perform popular, light-listening Bollywood numbers. My male vocal partner sings one that is popular at weddings:

'Baharo phool barsavo, mera meheboob aya he, (Oh Spring, let there be a shower of flowers, my beautiful sweetheart is approaching)'.

We find out the groom's mother and her siblings were brought up in Kenya. They request a Swahili song, so I sing: *'Malaika, Naku Penda Malaika,* (Angel, I love you, Angel)'.

After everyone has eaten, the dancing starts. My male colleague can sing in Punjabi and takes the stage by storm with *'Apna Punjab Hove,* (Let's go to Punjab).' He encourages the British audience to join in the *bhangra* dancing to this number and teaches them the famous 'change the light bulb move'. Smiles, embarrassment, laughter, stepping on the feet of others, hands and arms waving in the air – it's all happening on the dance floor.

I can sing in Hindi and Gujerati so we give the audience an eclectic cultural experience. I introduce the *'Garba',* which is a folk dance from Gujarat, like the *'Bhangra'* is a folk dance from Punjab. I demonstrate the two- and three-step moves in rhythm to my singing. I encourage the extroverted guests to invite the shy ones onto the dance floor. There are now no bums on seats, just tapping feet and clapping hands, mostly out of rhythm as I sing:

'Lejo taline tejo khali, (Clap once, step forward, and clap again).'

To add to the multicultural ambience of the evening, we persuade the bride's father to sing a song in Welsh after the speeches and so he renders the party a few lines of *'Ar hyd y Nos,* (All Through the Night),' to rapturous applause. It is a fitting end to a memorable evening for the bride and bridegroom and their guests.

It is a tiring journey home. We reflect on the evening as we chat. I tell my band-mates that, at first, I felt anxious about performing in public, but I am researching stress management for my thesis and that is helping me to overcome this anxiety.

I am gathering multiple forms of relaxation and breathing techniques to analyse. I practice these as I write my thesis and notice feeling more centred and calmer within myself. I find the passive progressive relaxation technique and alternate nostril breathing particularly effective. I begin to wake up twenty minutes early to practice my breathing techniques and do the same in my lunch breaks. These prove to be a lifeline and welcome release from the pressures of family, work and academic deadlines.

On top of all these pressures, my beloved Baapuji's health is failing during this time. He passes away two days after I have handed my thesis. I read the theories on loss posited by Kubler-Ross, Wordon, Silverman, and Klass, but no amount of academic study prepares you for a loss of this magnitude.

Initially, his loss casts its shadow over every part of our lives. As per Indian tradition, we have an open house for friends and relatives for the first week, which gives us an opportunity to share memories of Baapuji as we filter through our grief. We mimic his famous 'Chalto, Chalto (come on, come on)' phrase. We talk about his modesty, principles and the discipline with which he educated and provided a roof and comfort for his children. We make the okra fritters he loved. The reminiscing begins to shatter and splatter at the shadows.

The Indian traditions of spirituality and culture say death is a natural part of life. It is unrealistic to expect a parent to live forever. We believe that the soul is eternal and the physical body is reborn. Every day we will experience loss because change happens all the time. It may be a particularly unique sunrise or sunset, an item of jewellery with sentimental value that is lost or stolen, a delightful child who is suddenly an obstinate teenager, a job, a house or a loved one who was always strong but suddenly appears frail and indecisive. Change is normal, and when there is change, something is lost but also gained at the same time. We are not protected from the pain of the loss but encouraged to share it with each other. All this helps me to normalise and validate my grief. The seismic issue of mortality is painful to bear at first, however, the spectre gradually frizzles into oblivion as time moves forward.

After I graduate, I follow my studies with a couple of professional qualifications in stress management training, which give me a firm footing for working in the corporate world. Opportunities open up which enable me to travel across the country working. Eventually, I decide to leave my day job and I set up my own wellbeing consultancy. As the years of my part-time study, singing, and training progress, my confidence in myself blossoms too. One of the most vivid aspects of my personal growth here has been my transition to balancing my collective identity with my individual sense of self.

I say I was born into the transitional generation who had to work towards finding their individuality, influenced by Baa, who truly exuded the collective principles of Indian traditional culture, and my daughter who is growing up in the contemporary Western individualistic environment. When I got married, Baa said to me, *'Look after everyone in your new family.'* She did not say, *'Look after yourself first.'*

Unlike my European counterparts, I was born into a community that has a strong sense of family which merges into a collective group identity. Women especially may be conditioned to put the needs of the family before their own. Even though I was given every freedom by the family I was born into, I was still influenced by the wider community's conditioning. One of the hardest aspects of my growth has been to let go of the guilt and learn to balance my needs as an individual with those of the extended family I married into.

All through these hurdles, my husband helps me in my parenting and household tasks while I study and train. Again, I am blessed to have my parents' love replicated by a life-partner who loves me unconditionally. My education assists me in highlighting my needs, and I am supported in this by my children and my peers. Not only that, my children are doing well in school and growing up to be fine, caring, compassionate human beings. As I approach my big four-o birthday, I find that I am finding myself and coming into my own as a person. It has been quite a tumultuous personal journey, but eventually, after losing sight of it for a few years, I am happy. I feel at home.

***

Kenya has been far from my radar, though, until a series of conversations with my friend Jane brings all my memories flooding back.

CHAPTER 9

KENYA IN THE NEWS

BIRMINGHAM, ENGLAND, 1995

I am forty now. I am sitting with my friend Jane in an Indian restaurant. We are tucking into curry and *naan* bread. Jane has now acquired a taste for chilli-laden spicy food. In fact, she orders the *vindaloo*, which I cannot stomach. As Kenya has been in the news, we re-visit a conversation that we had when we first met five years ago.

***

She sees my Indian looks and hears my faintly accented speech. She asks,

'Which part of India are you from and how long have you been in England?'

This is a common inquisition I get on a first meeting and I immediately think,

'*Here we go again.*'

'I have only been to India for one short holiday,' I say. 'I was born in Kenya.'

'Oh, so you came here as a refugee?'

'No, I came because I am a British passport-holder, as were my dad and grandad.'

'Oh, really? How's that?'

I tell her I am asked this question umpteen times, often when I meet a new British person.

***

We begin to talk about the day's news coverage of the political issues in Kenya.

'I realise now I was actually born during the political uprising seeking independence from the British Empire. For half my time in Kenya, it was a British colony, and the other half, a free country.' I tell Jane as she asks me about my life in Kenya. 'Growing up, I heard the words "*Uhuru, Mau Mau, Kenyatta*" bandied about, but never understood their meaning. Thika, where I was born, is in the central region of the country where a lot of the fighting was taking place, but I have no memory of any of this. I later found out that there was a lot of fear around, but my parents protected us well from it and I did not sense any of this.'

As I take a bite of my scrumptious stuffed pepper, I see the look of fascination in Jane's face urging me to continue.

'Kenyans and Indians had similar experiences in their quest for independence. The British colonial powers used the divide-and-rule approach in both countries. In India, they played on the tension and divide between Hindus and Muslims; in Kenya, between the different tribal groups, especially the Kikuyus, Lous, and Samburus. Gandhi in India tried the non-violent approach. Despite that, there was much violence and loss of life, especially during the partition of India and Pakistan in 1947.'

I pause as I see the brightness in Jane's eyes fade, a lump forming in her throat. She tries to swallow her piece of *naan* soaked in chicken vindaloo but coughs and splutters instead. I pass her a glass of water. She takes a few sips and composes herself before responding, 'This is awful. You can say I am ignorant, but, truly, I had no idea about any of this.' She gulps and clears her throat again. 'I need to know more about all this, maybe do some reading.'

I notice the fingers on her left-hand reach to her blonde, shoulder-length hair and entwine with the ends spontaneously. We search for some information and books on Google before parting for the evening.

***

A few weeks later, Jane comes over to my house for a day together to continue our discussion. After the usual catch-up about work and family, she says she wants to share with me the reading she has been doing on the British Empire, Kenya and India.

'Let me start at the beginning. I will read to you what I have gathered.' She settles down on her favourite part of my couch and begins to read:

'In the 900s, Arab merchants arrived and established trading centres along the eastern coast of Africa. Over the subsequent eight centuries, they succeeded in converting many of the inhabitants of Kenya to Islam. Some Arabs settled in the area and intermarried with local groups. Portuguese explorer Vasco da Gama landed at the port of Mombasa in Kenya in 1498 after discovering a sailing route around the Cape of Good Hope. The Portuguese colonised much of the region, but the Arabs managed to evict them in 1729.

'In the mid-1800s, European explorers stumbled upon Mount Kilimanjaro and Mount Kenya and began to take an interest in the natural resources of eastern Africa. Christian missionaries came as well, drawn by the large numbers of prospective converts. Britain gradually increased its dominance in the region, and in 1884-1885, what would become Kenya was named a British protectorate by the Congress of Berlin, which divided the African continent amongst various European powers. Within the British Protectorate of East Africa, the British constructed a railway to connect the ports on Kenya's coast to the land-locked territory that is is now Uganda.'

At this point, I add, 'Since India at this time was also a British colony, the British brought Indian workers over to build this railway – this is how the Indian story in Kenya began. Indian labour was transported to many British colonies, Guyana is another example. Half a million Indians were later enlisted to fight in the British army in the Second World War and thousands died for a country, other than their own, halfway around the world from their homes. But all that is another story.'

'Oh really?' Jane's eyes cloud over as she takes this in. The left-fingers on her left hand twiddled with her hair again – this is something she subconsciously does when she's upset.

'Please carry on, Jane, this is helping me to connect some dots.' I nod to the pieces of paper in her right hand.

'The increasing economic opportunities brought thousands of British settlers who displaced many Africans, often forcing them to live on reservations. The Africans resisted. The Kikuyu tribe in particular put up a strong fight, but they were defeated by the superior military power of the British. During the early twentieth century, the British colonisers forced the Africans to work their farms in virtual slavery and kept the upper-hand by making it illegal for them to grow their own food. In the early 1920s, a Kikuyu named Harry Thuku began to encourage rebellion amongst his tribe and founded the East Africa Association. He was arrested by the British in 1922, provoking a popular protest to which the British reacted violently, killing twenty-five people in what came to be called "The Nairobi Massacre".'

Jane stops reading and stares at the sheet in front of her. I cannot see the hazel in her eyes as they moisten and fill up. Her peach lipsticked lips curve down at the corners. After a long, husky, outlet of breath, she exclaims,

'Oh, Christ. This does not make me very proud of my British heritage. I bet half this country hasn't got a clue about any of this.'

'Half the world, maybe, because I had no clue of these details either. I hate to upset you more, Jane, but in India there are many similar stories that are much, much worse.'

'Yes, I watched the film *"Gandhi"* last week with my husband...'

She goes quiet again and I wait for her to finish her sentence. When she continues this time, it is in a softer achy tone.

'I am going to watch it again with my kids and talk to them about some of this.'

She raises her head slowly and holds my gaze with a look of guilt and shame. I get up, cross over to the sofa, and hold my arms out, inviting her for a hug. We hold each other in a forgiving embrace, my way of reassurance that she had no part to play in all this.

Then I do what the British do whenever something gets difficult and uncomfortable: I offer her a cup of tea.

'Oh yes, please,' she says in a lighter tone. 'Shall we have your boiled Indian *chai* instead? I prefer that to English tea,' and adds, 'I'll pop to the loo while you do that.'

We enjoy our tea and snacks before she continues with the history lesson.

'Desire for self-rule continued to build and in 1944 the Kenya African Union, a nationalist political party, was founded. In 1946, the Kikuyu leader Jomo Kenyatta returned from sixteen years living in England and began agitating for Kenyan independence. Back on his home soil, he was elected president of the Kenya African Union. His rallying cry was... "A...h...r..." How do you pronounce this? I will spell it out, "U-H-U-R-U".'

'Oo-hoo-roo,' I help. 'It is Swahili for "freedom".' She repeats after me, 'Oo-hoo-roo', then continues.

'While Kenyatta advocated peaceful rebellion, other Kikuyu formed secret groups that pledged to win independence by whatever means necessary, including violence. In the early 1950s, members of these groups, known as "Mau Mau", murdered 32 white civilians, 167 police officers, and 1,819 Kikuyu who disagreed with the Mau Mau's absolutist stance.'

Jane reaches for a sip of *chai* as I interject,

'I was born in 1955, which is right in the middle of this political rebellion. I heard the adults use these words, "Uhuru", "Kenyatta", "Mau Mau", but we carried on playing in the grass square outside our house with the neighbouring kids, oblivious to the dangers.'

'That is incredible,' she says and carries on,

'In retaliation for these murders, the British killed a total of 11,503 Mau Mau and their sympathisers. British justice also included displacing entire tribes and interning them in barbed-wire camps. Despite Kenyatta's public denouncement of the Mau Mau, the British tried him as a Mau Mau leader and imprisoned him for nine years.'

'I remember the adults' discussions about Kenyatta being in jail,' I add.

'While Kenyatta was in prison, two other leaders stepped in to fill his place: Tom Mboya, of the Luo tribe, was the more moderate of the two, and had the support of Western nations; Oginga Odinga, also a Luo, was more radical and had the support of the Soviet bloc. They were united in their goal to give African-Kenyans the right to vote, and in 1957, Africans won their first representation in the colonial government when eight African-Kenyans were elected to seats in the legislature. By 1961, they constituted a majority of the legislative body.'

'I was six years old then, oblivious to the quest for an independent Kenya and the political storm that was fast gathering momentum,' I intrude.

'In 1960, at the Lancaster House Conference in London, the British approved Kenyan independence, setting the date for

December, 1963. Kenyatta, released from prison in 1961, became prime minister of a newly independent Kenya on 12 December,1963, and was elected to the office of president the following year. Although he was a Kikuyu, one of Kenyatta's primary goals was to overcome tribalism. He appointed members of different ethnic groups to his government, including Mboya and Odinga. His slogan became "Harambee", meaning "Let's all pull together".'

'There is a song we used to sing in school,' I say and start to sing whatever lyrics I can recall:

> *'Harambe Harambe, harambee harambee*
> *tuimbe pamoja*
> *tujenge serikali.'*

Jane joins in, giggling and struggling with the pronunciation. The door to the living room opens and my daughter pops her head in. 'Judging by the sound of singing and giggles, you two seem to be having a great time.'

'Yes, we are,' we both reply in unison. 'You are most welcome to join us.'

My daughter shakes her head and disappears into the kitchen.

'So, where were we?' Jane picks up the sheet of paper to continue and I am intrigued to learn more. All this was happening on my doorstep as I am growing up and I did not have a clue!

'In 1966, Odinga abdicated his position as vice-president in order to start his own political party. Kenyatta, fearing cultural divisiveness, arrested Odinga and outlawed all political parties except his own. On 5 July, 1969, Tom Mboya was assassinated and tensions between the Luo and the Kikuyu increased.'

'That was when I was sitting my secondary school mock-exams. You know, we were taught with the same English education system and examining boards as students here in the UK. We had Indian, African, and English teachers. Some of the English teachers were Peace Corp Volunteers. I got a distinction in my finals.'

67

Jane laughs. 'Okay, Clever-clogs, tell me about school in Kenya another time. Today, I want to get through this.'

'Sure, will do, go on.'

'In elections later that year, Kenyatta won re-election and political stability returned. Overall, the fifteen years of Kenyatta's presidency were a time of economic and political stability. When Kenyatta died on 22 August, 1978, the entire nation mourned his death. The vice-president, Daniel arap Moi, took over.'

I interrupt Jane again. 'That's the year I got married, in England. I got married in the May and Kenyatta died in the August. I must have heard it in the news but was too preoccupied adjusting to marriage and living with my in-laws.'

'Really? How long did you live with your in-laws? You are brave, Hansa, I would not have survived a week.'

'Well, it is an Indian tradition, and it has many advantages if you get on with each other. You can save for a mortgage, no childcare costs if you have a young family, dinner is on the table when you get home from work, and so on. When I married, it was the expected thing to do and you would be seen as the baddie if you moved out before the house outgrew the family. But now, it is not so. Most young Indian couples have their own place before getting married. I do not expect my son and his future wife to live with me after marriage.'

Jane says, 'We'll have to come back to that another time if we are to get through this today.'

I ask, 'Yes, what time do you have to get back?'

'About six-ish, so we have an hour or so. Here we go.' And she carries on reading aloud:

'Arap Moi initially promised to improve on Kenyatta's government by ending corruption and releasing political prisoners. While he made some progress on these goals, Arap Moi gradually restricted people's liberty, outlawing all political parties except his own. In 1982, a military coup attempted to overthrow him, but the coup was unsuccessful.'

'That's the year my beautiful daughter was born. I was too busy with work, in-laws, and a hyper three-year-old son to pay much attention to Kenyan politics.'

She continues, 'Arap Moi did away with secret ballots and several times changed election dates spontaneously to keep people from voting. Western nations responded by demanding that Kenya hold multi-party elections if they wanted to continue to receive foreign aid, and in December, 1992, Arap Moi won re-election despite widespread complaints of bribery and ballot tampering.'

She looks up from her piece of paper in her hand and adds, 'And that's what's been in the news lately. The Kenyan economy floundering, inflation skyrocketing, the Kenyan currency devalued by fifty per cent.'

'From what we have gathered, under Kenyatta the country had stability and gained economic progress as well as Western respect, but it sounds like, after that, it went the other way...'

'Yes, that's the way it feels... There's just a bit more left. Do we have time to finish?' Jane asks. She glances at her watch and answers her own question, 'I have fifteen minutes, just enough,' and carries on.

'The Kikuyu are the largest tribe in the highlands and tend to dominate the nation's politics. While the Kikuyu have enjoyed the most power in the post-independence government, they were also the hardest-hit by brutal British policies during the colonial period. The Kikuyu traditionally had an antagonistic relationship with the Masai, and the two groups often raided each other's villages and cattle herds. At the same time, there was a good deal of intermarriage and cultural exchange between the two groups.'

Jane pauses to hear my experiences on any of this. After a few seconds, I say:

'Our milkman, he was called Chhege, he was Kikuyu. My history teacher in secondary school was Luo. I had Kikuyu girls in my class at secondary school. One who sat next to me in class, Wanjiru, I remember fondly – she had a wicked sense of humour. She told me the Kikuyu were matriarchal, power in the hands of women, before men overthrew them. She said she was named after one of the nine Kikuyu Tribe's founders. Also, I saw the Masai people many times and have photos. Maybe I will show you those another time... Anyway, go on.'

'But relations among various other ethnic groups are also fraught with tension, and this has been a major obstacle in creating a united Kenya. These conflicts are partly a legacy of colonial rule when the British exacerbated ethnic tensions by playing groups off against one another in order to reinforce their own power. For example, under British rule, different ethnic groups were confined to specific geographic areas. Tensions between the various tribes still continue to this day.'

Jane stops. 'Oops, it's ten past six, I have to stop and go pick up Mike from work.' She gathers her bag and gives me a quick cuddle as she says, 'I've not got all of the India, Kenya, England connection yet. Need to do some more of this. Give you a bell next week?'' She rushes out the door, her voice trailing behind her: 'Bye, Sweetie... Will call you.'

I stay awake most of that night reflecting on how oblivious I was as a child in my one-mile- and ten-mile-radius worlds to the tumultuous events that were going on in Thika.

CHAPTER 10

INDIA, KENYA, AND ENGLAND CONNECTIONS

Later that week, it is a cold winter evening and we are all sat by the fire in the living room, snacking on *garam garam*, *bhajiya*, and boiled masala *chai*. My children have become inquisitive about my Kenya-India connection. I am not surprised as I have been jabbering about it all week since Jane came over.

'So, Mum, how come you were born in Kenya but grandad was Indian? How come we were born in the UK?' my son asks.

I give a summary of the explanation I gave Jane and top it up with more family history gained from childhood stories told to me by my Fai.

'Ah... That's why your brother's house in Birmingham is called "Chhaya Plot". What a lovely way to keep that connection,' my daughter remarks.

'India and Kenya were both British colonies, as you have gathered. There was a migration of labour between the colonies.

The Indian population mostly came to Kenya in the early twentieth century to work on the railways and roads. Many later became merchants and store owners.'

'Wow, Mum, you never told us any of this before,' my son says excitedly.

'You never asked. Like I never asked my father, and now I wonder why? It just never occurred to any of us. I suppose that was our normality and we assumed everyone was the same in the world. How wrong we all are.'

'Are you seeing Auntie Jane again?' my daughter asks in anticipation.

'Yes, in a few weeks,' I say.

***

Later that month, I meet up with Jane again. She has been reading up more about colonial rule in Kenya and India and we continue our discussion.

'The Indians were the in-betweeners in Kenya under colonial rule – the underdogs to the westerners and top-dogs to the Africans. They contributed greatly to the economy with their diligent work ethic and entrepreneurial flair, but in 1967, when I was in secondary school, Kenyatta started a drive to Africanise Kenya. First preference was given to African-Kenyans for jobs and public posts. Indian-Kenyans began to feel marginalised, and, as colonial British citizens, gradually started migrating to Britain. Some left Kenya when their jobs and livelihoods became precarious. My older brother and sister came here for higher education when it came time to go to university.

'Many British politicians resisted this flow of Indian-Kenyans into the United Kingdom and sent a delegation to India to persuade them to take them instead. But India said that they had migrated to Kenya under British colonial rule and, as British passport-holders, were Britain's responsibility. Some agreed with India's stance and accepted Indian-Kenyans' entry to Britain, recognising and honouring the Asian contribution to The British Empire.'

'Has that got anything to do with the exodus of Indian refugees in 1972? I remember it all on the news. One of the rehabilitation camps was not far from where my sister lived, in the south of England,' Jane asks.

I shake my head vehemently, 'No, Jane, many people confuse this. Kenyan-Indians came to Britain voluntarily because of the gradual change in their economic situation under Kenyatta. They were not forced out in a massive ninety-day exodus as the Ugandan-Indians were by Idi Amin. Kenyan-Indians were not put in internment camps. They settled in Britain by themselves, often helped by relatives who had arrived earlier. The reason my family settled in Birmingham is because my Fai was already here. My cousin, Motabaa's son, was one of the first of our family to come to Britain, followed by my older siblings.'

'It is widely understood that the purpose of the Commonwealth Immigration Act of 1968 was in fact to deny non-white Brits their citizenship rights, following heavy petitioning to stem the tide of Kenyan-Asians entering Britain. It is worth noting that upon the UK's entry to the EU in 1973, the European Court of Human Rights ruled that the Commonwealth Immigration Act of 1968 was racially discriminatory and robbed British-Asians of equal citizenship rights, in violation of the European Convention on Human Rights of 1950 to which the UK was one of the first signatories. This is why there was a delay in my parents and younger siblings joining us. When I say I came in 1971, people often ask me if I was part of the exodus and I have to explain all of this.'

'So, Hansa, what puzzles me is this: why did your father choose to come to Britain, the country of his oppressors both in India and Kenya?'

This is a loaded question and I have to think for a few minutes. Maybe if my father had been a businessman we would have stayed in Kenya. If he had been an Indian nationalist, we may have moved to India. In the end, I say, 'I can only guess at the answer. I was never privy to the conversations of my parents and their friends about their choice of country. Knowing my father, and speaking to my brothers, I am sure he made the choice he did because he wanted the best education for his children, like his father before him.'

And it's true, I can't ever remember either of my parents expressing any resentment towards the British or Kenyans. They lived a simple life and did what they believed was best for their children.

'Even if they held any resentment, which I doubt they did, they taught us to forgive. I remember my mum saying to me: "Forgiveness is never about letting the other person off the hook. It's more about letting go of the burden of holding on to your anger indefinitely because this could have repercussions on your mental and physical health".'

Jane quips in, 'If you think about what's going on in the world, it seems more like revenge than forgiveness.'

'Well, most of us have witnessed a scenario when one person starts shouting, the other shouts back, anger escalates, and sometimes things become physical. But imagine the opposite, one person shouts and displays aggression and the other talks back calmly and with kindness. The chances are that the anger dissipates, breaking the confrontational cycle. Acting from compassion is more effective than acting from pity or hate. I did a lot of work on anger management at university. The angry other person is still an individual with worth and value, we all are. If we strive to believe that nobody is the enemy because we are all connected in this way, then it makes sense to seek a common solution instead of trying to prove we are right or better than others.

'There are many Mahatma Gandhi quotes I can give as inspiration here:

'Don't be angry until you have walked in the other person's shoes for a few miles.'

'An eye for an eye makes the whole world blind.'

'When you point a finger at someone, you have three fingers pointing back at you.'

'I believe my parents were humanistic. My siblings and I were brought up to see good in all people, to look for commonalities rather than differences. We were brought up to be loyal and grateful, and to give back to society rather than only take. We never claimed benefits, we worked hard for our future. We were taught not to judge others. I am sure my parents would have held on to those same values and loved and respected whatever country we ended up in... Instead of looking at what is wrong with others, we need to look at how we can become better human beings and make a difference to people and the planet, because ultimately, Jane, we are all outsiders to someone.'

'Yes, I agree,' says Jane.

'And there is always another perspective,' I add. 'I had an English colleague at work whose parents lived in Kenya during colonial rule. They worked hard on the land they owned to build the local community and, like my parents, they had to leave behind everything when the policy of Africanisation was introduced. The British built the Kenyan roads and railways and transformed much of the land for modern agricultural use. Kenya enjoys the fruits of this. We should say the country was built together by the British, Indians, and Africans."

We stop for our usual *chai* and snacks break. While I am in the kitchen preparing this, it gives me time to reflect on what we have been discussing, and I share my reflections with Jane as I return to the lounge:

'What strikes me now as we talk about all this is that while the British were taking over land for the British Empire, its newly-acquired subjects were sprouting their own histories, rich and dynamic and soulful histories, under the banner of the British flag. British subjects like my family sowed their seeds of culture and commerce wherever they went and these are flourishing and blooming all over the world, but I doubt many people know much about this, I don't think you will find this in the British history books.'

Jane is looking out of the window as she listens. 'Yes, Hansa, your story could well be a work of fiction, but in actuality it's as real as that setting sun over there, and that moon waiting to take its place.'

She turns to me. 'I think you should write a book about all this. It is much needed. I have looked in The British Library history archives and there is an absence of first-hand narratives like yours. Most of the colonial historical accounts were written by the British, from the perspective of the British themselves.'

I am not sure about writing a book, but Jane persists, 'What strikes me about all this is that you and your family are as much British as me, if not more.'

I smile and tell her, 'I remember this robust wrangle we had in our team at work during the Queen's Silver Jubilee in 1977. There was this debate going on in the media whether there should be public money spent on the celebrations. I had only been in this country for six years and I was beaming with pride, having watched the celebrations on television and thoroughly enjoyed our street party. Some of my anti-royal colleagues, born and brought up in this country, did not feel the same. It was ironic, as well as comical. You see, living under British rule, we grew up being part of the ups and downs of the royal family. In Kenya, it was a public holiday when the Queen's children were born. The day Prince Andrew was born, I was five years old and I remember being part of a street party and people talking about a baby boy being born to the Queen. Everything shut down for the celebrations. I also recall my cousin being ecstatic because he had been in Nairobi on Kenyan

Independence Day and had seen Prince Phillip in person. We were taught the British national anthem in school... Do you know it?'

'"God Save the Queen"? Oh, Yes I do. But, I mean, it's not very exciting, it's only two verses.'

'Oh, on the contrary, Jane, there are many verses and with admirable sentiments! Except the final one about "crushing rebellious Scots" – I don't think anyone sings that one anymore. Shall we have a go?'

'God save our gracious
Queen,
Long live our noble Queen,
God save the Queen!
Send her victorious,
Happy and glorious,
Long to reign over us,
God save the Queen!

'O Lord our God arise,
Scatter our enemies,
And make them fall!
Confound their politics,
Frustrate their knavish tricks,
On Thee our hopes we fix,
God save us all!

'From every latent foe,
From the assassins blow,
God save the Queen!
O'er her thine arm extend,
For Britain's sake defend,
Our mother, prince, and
friend,
God save the Queen!

'Thy choicest gifts in store,
On her be pleased to pour,
Long may she reign!
May she defend our laws,
And ever give us cause,
To sing with heart and voice,
God save the Queen!

'Not in this land alone,
But be God's mercies known,
From shore to shore!
Lord make the nations see,
That men should brothers be,
And form one family,
The wide world ov'er.

Jane raises her right hand and wiggles her fingers, trying to imitate the Queen's signature wave, and says 'Why not? Yes, let's go into the British patriotic zone!' And we begin to sing: 'My dear Jane, you would make a brilliant Queen with that wave! Talking of the Queen, one of our local community leaders, Mr. Devshi Mepa Shah, was awarded an M.B.E in recognition of his social and charitable work in the '50s.'

Jane replies, 'And here's me, still in the same house I was born in, and still in the same town, apart from a few touristy holidays to Europe and one trip to America. I like the royal family, though, so at least we share that,' she winks. 'When I retire, I plan to catch up on seeing the world, maybe visit some of these Commonwealth countries... I would love to go on a safari! Have you seen the film "Safari", from the '50s? The wildlife is spectacular and unbelievable.'

I have not just seen the film 'Safari'. Rather, I have been on one.

CHAPTER 11

TIME WARP

THIKA, KENYA, 2001

I am forty-six now. My son, twenty-two, has just finished university, and my daughter is nineteen. Life is surging ahead, and I am playing catch up. My husband and I want our children to learn about our roots and experience our childhood, so we set off to Kenya for a holiday.

We step off the plane and onto the soil of Nairobi and my heart churns and wrenches with nostalgia. For my children, it is the excitement of Africa, an alien continent and culture, as well as curiosity about their parents' childhood years.

A distant relative, Rajesh, has invited us to stay in his home and he picks us up from the airport. A sea of African faces whish past the car windows as we drive to his house. In the years following independence, before I took off to England, Kenya was a fairly law-abiding country in my experience. From what we hear from Rajesh, and what we see, it does not appear this way now. He tells us stories of corruption and political infighting.

The next morning, we are asked to take off all our jewellery and watches before leaving the house, for fear of being mugged. I think back to my trips to Nairobi with Motabaa and Motabapuji when we would stroll happily in the bazaars and restaurants of Nairobi, without fear of being robbed. I would clutch Motabaa's hand and follow her as she meandered from one stall to the next, asking Motabapuji's opinion prior to purchasing little items. This is in sharp contrast to seeing the security personnel now guarding the area for the safety of the shoppers.

'What about the restaurants,' I ask Rajesh, 'do these have security guards too?' He says there are still some areas that are safe for us to eat at tonight.

The next day, we set off to Masai Mara Safari Park. On the way is the Great Rift Valley Viewpoint. The valley runs the length of Kenya, a geographical trench six thousand kilometres long, from northern Syria, through central and east Africa, down to Mozambique in southern Africa. It is believed to have been formed twenty million years ago when the Earth's crust ripped apart. Not wanting to miss out on this sight, we stop, walk up to the fenced edge of the Viewpoint, and gaze across at the humongous space below, unending both to the left and the right. The brown, green, grey, and in-between colours of the land and the hills shy away from us behind the mist and clouds.

The aroma of crackling corn on the cob veers us to the street vendor a few yards from our spot.

'*Jambo Bwana*,' the vendor greets us cheerfully.

The corn on the cob, sprinkled with salt, chilli and lemon, takes me back into my one-mile world in Thika and I tell my children about Kamau and my afterschool treats with my classmates.

'Mum, so you never had crisps and chocolate as treats?' my daughter asks, with a look that says: '*You have not lived if you have not tasted crisps*'.

'No,' I say. 'It was fresh street food. I had chocolates when I went out with Motabaa and Motabapuji but cannot remember having them at home.' Once again, I am reminded of my split young life – poor kid on weekdays and rich kid at weekends.

Later, we are welcomed to the Masai village by a group of young men. They are dressed in traditional orange cloths crisscrossing their slim bodies, white paint marks on their faces, and wear large round earrings that circle the whole elongated earlobe. They break out in a Masai song and dance and we are enticed to join in.

'Would you like to see the village?' one asks us in English.

We nod and one of them leads the way. The village is a scattering of round mud huts with flat roofs made of assorted metal sheets. We stoop through the entrance of one to see a wood fire in the left corner, leather sheets as beds, and a small fenced area to the right that has a calf suckling away with its mother – all in a four-metre-radius space.

'They live in such a small place, and do not have much,' my son remarks as he smiles and waves to a group of women and children chattering in the shade of a tree, 'but they look happy and contented.'

We drive up to the Masai Mara Lodge that night – apparently, the Queen was visiting here when she received the news of the death of her father, King George VI – and the next day, we head off on safari.

The safari is unbelievably breath-taking!

'Hey look, there are some zebras!' my son shouts in excitement.

My children feast on this first sight of a live zebra. From only a few yards away, we also see wildebeest, lions, deer, and elephants, all in their natural habitat. That night, we stay in a tent on the edge of the animals' terrain and listen to their night sounds. Hearing them at night is scary! As is having go behind bushes to go to the loo. We later see an elephant drop a big poo twenty times the size we humans are capable of. But the most beautiful sight on safari – the highlight – has to be the row of majestic giraffes walking into the sunset towards the end of our third day.

We drive up to the Lake Naivasha National Park next to see white hippos, crocodiles, and the spectacular famous flamingos flying over the lake.

At the hotel, close to Thomson's Falls, we are entertained with Swahili and English live-music and are startled when the band suddenly springs into a Bollywood Hindi song. This takes me back to the Indian singing game 'Antakshari' which we play the next day to pass the time on our journey to our next destination. Antakshari is a popular addition to Indian parties, long journeys, and social gatherings. You begin with a song and opposite participants sing the next song starting with the sound that the previous song ends in. My husband sings one that is apt for the magnificence of our surroundings at that moment:

'And I think to myself...what a wonderful world...'

We are playing boys-versus-girls so my daughter and I have to come up with a song that starts with the sound 'D'. We follow him with a Bollywood song:

'Ddafli wale...dafli baja...mere ghunghroo bulate hea...aaa, me nachu, to nacha...' (I dance to the rhythm of your drum beat and my anklets.)

The boys have to sing a song beginning with the sound 'CHA'.

And so on. The game goes on for the next hour.

'We win,' my daughter says. 'You guys cheated, twice.'

'No, we did not. You girls started with the wrong sound quite a few times.'

We agree to call it a draw.

That evening, back at the hotel, the band plays the famous African song,

'Jambo...jambo bwanaa habari gani mazuri sana', during dinner. Throughout the holiday so far, our three cultures, Kenyan, Indian and English, have entwined simultaneously, like the three strands of the enchanting, long, dark-haired plait of the lady on the next table. To me and my husband, this exposure feels as natural as breathing, and we are delighted when the children embrace it too. We are all happy. We all feel at home.

Our next destination is Mount Kenya. From our room, I see the mountain peaking beyond the lush garden complex of the hotel, dotted with bougainvillea and the odd peacock boasting its stunning feathers. It is peaceful and relaxing here after the hustle of the past few days, with just the mountain, us, and the peacock showing off.

The next day we cross the Equator. For some, this is a momentous event in their lives, but my heart is hitting at my rib cage for another reason – we are approaching Thika and my ten-mile-radius world. I have that grin on my face that nobody can wipe off, no matter how hard they try.

We visit Fourteen Falls, Thika Falls, and finally my childhood friend, Chania Falls.

'Mum, you were so blessed to have been brought up in such beautiful surroundings,' my daughter says, giving me a big affectionate hug.

'You haven't seen anything yet!' I quip. 'Wait until we climb down close to the waterfalls.'

We go, just like my siblings and I did as children, through the Blue Post Hotel gardens, which look just the same, down the slippery rocky stairway to more rocks swished and kissed by the waterfall. Someone has added a horizontal tree trunk as a makeshift bench between two high rocks, but apart from that it is all the same as it has been in my mind's eye all these years. We try sitting on different rocks to catch the best view, dip our feet in the cool water as it rushes past our feet, and play the same games of *'Splash water at each other'* and *'Who can throw the pebbles highest'* into the waterfall. I think I am dreaming.

We end our visit with a coffee and snack at the hotel, this time with my children instead of my siblings.

I have somersaults in my stomach now, as well as the thumping heart and ear-to-ear grin, because we are driving to the house of my one-mile-radius world!

We walk through the short alleyway and knock on the (still blue) door. No-one opens for a while and I wonder if people still live here. Then the door creaks open and a face from thirty-plus years ago appears: Shobna was our neighbour all those years ago and I am flabbergasted that she still lives here. She recognizes me instantly and welcomes us in.

It all feels surreal, like I am in a time-warp.

The house has the same blue doors, blue window frames, same veranda adjoining the small kitchen and bathroom, and the same four-foot-square allotment and pebble yard with clothes line running across. But there is no courgette plant – it has dried out – and the jasmine shrub has been replaced with a pomegranate tree. And there is no buzzing family with a mother rushing around to tend to her children and father coming home after a hard day's work. The rooms are now used for storage by a nearby business.

We exchange news on our respective lives before Shobna picks a few pomegranates and packs them in a bag as a gift. Her life has not changed all these years and yet ours is another world apart.

We say our goodbyes and head for the temple. As we cross the road, I try to recall the number of times I crossed this road as a child. My heart sinks a little with sadness as I do so – my beloved grass square is not much of a grass square now. We pick our way through the unkempt, uneven, non-grassy patches and overgrown shrubs.

We enter the temple and it looks just as I remember it. We walk up to the far end to the altar and the gleaming, colourful deities and I find what I am searching for: the single bronze bells hanging on either side of the worship area, the bells we used to ring with glee after the race to the temple after play-time.

'I used to compete with my siblings and friends to get to the bells first to ring them during *Aarti*,' I tell my children.

'I bet they got here first most of the time, Mum,' my son jokes. I give him an affectionate soft clip on the ear and ring the bell once with delight. The bell is rung a single ring during worship, but during *Aarti,* they ring for the duration of the ritual. I bow to the deities and catch the eye of the female deity who still bears the same kind knowing look and soft reassuring comforting smile. The same as the little version of her in my shrine in my front reception room at home in England. I give gratitude like I do every day for her guidance to serve my life's purpose in the best way possible.

Our next stop is the school, which looks the same but run-down. We walk around the grounds and I point out my classes, the headmaster's office, the play-areas and school hall at the end. The secondary school is behind the playground, through the gates. Again, not much has changed except for the lack of maintenance. At the time of writing, my older brother is working on an alumni project to raise funds for the school, especially for the provision of computers and other technology.

We drive up to Section Nine with its affluent detached houses.

'Mum, why is this area called "Section Nine"? Are there other sections?' my son asks.

'I do remember being told by a teacher that he had seen a very old map with all of Thika's sections, but since the others had disappeared and this was the last one, the name "Section Nine" seems to have stuck.'

We go past Motabaa's old house, and then the block of flats where they lived after Motabapuji's retirement. I notice the area is now more African, we do not spot any Indians.

'Everything is the same, but run-down,' I say.

'Mum, you sound like a broken record,' my daughter says with a laugh.

'Just like the *"I want chips, I want chips"* record you kids played on our holiday in India,' I joke back.

My broken record continues as we drive past the post office, the local park, and the row of businesses along the 'high street', as we say in England. The businesses are now owned by Africans, but I spot the odd Indian person walking out of a shop and getting into their car.

Our last stop is Mombasa, the coastal tourist hot-spot where my husband grew up.

His family moved to Britain under similar circumstances to mine. He gives us a tour of the house where he grew up, the neighbourhood and his friends' houses, his school, the cinema, and, lastly, where he played with his friends on the beach. We go past Fort Jesus, which was erected by the first Portuguese settlers. All through our trip, he has been craving his favourite and much-fabled roadside treat: cassava crisps. We stop wherever we spot these so he can tuck in with gusto.

We spend our last few days relaxing and sunning ourselves in the luxury hotel with indoor and outdoor pools, palm trees, and adjoining beach. We enjoy the multicultural cuisine. It is our last chance to tuck into more of the *ugali* and *sukuma wiki* which take me back to our carefree days with Kuende and Wanjiku and Mrs. Nyame's hospitality.

On the last day of our holiday, I am sunning on the balcony of our hotel room when I suddenly let out an almighty scream. My husband hears this on the beach a few yards away and runs up the stairs two at a time.

'What is it, what's the matter, are you okay?' he asks, panting, as he gets to the balcony.

Perched on the wall is a monkey, staring at me. I think he is telling me he will pounce on me any second.

Two hotel security staff appear, joining the drama, and shoo away the monkey into a nearby tree. Phew!

On the plane back to England, my husband asks, 'Are you okay? You seem a bit edgy.'

And I am. It does not feel right. All that pleasure, amazing sights and scenes, animals, taste-bud-busting international cuisine, international music, nostalgia, fun, laughter, memorable bonding time with my family, and then a menacing monkey steals the limelight at the end!

But the next moment, I am dreaming of my home in Thika. Baa is sitting in the kitchen, rolling *rotis*. Baapuji is reading out to her the list of groceries she has bought on credit, he wants to check it before he pays the bill. The grocery list needs to be worked out carefully with the other household expenses such as school fees, clothes, shoes, rent and electric bill. I feel proud of Baa and Baapuji, they budgeted very carefully to make sure we were provided with all our basic needs. And they valued education, making sure school fees were paid bang on time even if it meant other things would have to be gone without.

I wake up with a jolt – the passenger behind me is snoring. I think over the values my parents instilled in all their children, the values I am aiming to instil in mine, and my grandchildren when they come along: love for people and the planet, priority of education, integrity, humility, benevolence. The trip back to Thika has reminded me of all the essential life lessons I learned from my parents and I smile at myself as a wave of peace and tranquillity sweeps through my body. In the end, it is Baa and Baapuji who have had the final say! Life is one long lesson and I still have a lot more to learn.

CHAPTER 12

EASTERN LESSONS FROM THE WESTERNERS

BIRMINGHAM, ENGLAND, 2002

I am forty-seven now. A question from Susan, an English colleague, shakes my world profoundly. I have a few minor health issues and have been low on energy lately and I ask Susan for advice. She is a natural health practitioner who shares my work premises.

'It is possible there is a block in one of your *chakras*...' she says.

'Sorry, what did you say?' I ask puzzled.

'The seven main *chakras*, in our body. Maybe one of yours is blocked?'

'I don't understand, what are "*chakras*"?' I ask.

She responds with a shocked look on her face. 'Hansa, you are of Indian origin, how do you not know about the *chakras*?'

I am shocked too. The truth is that many Indian-origin people have no clue about their traditional medicinal heritage and rely exclusively on allopathic medicines during bouts of illness. The irony is that I am now learning about *chakras* and Indian health traditions in Britain from an English colleague!

Susan teaches me that *'chakras'* are energy centres within the human body that help to regulate all its processes, from organ function, to the immune system, and emotions. She tells me we can commonly count seven *chakras* positioned throughout our body, from the base of the spine to the crown of the head, and each controls particular parts of the body, energising particular organs and bringing harmony within the body. If any of these *chakras* are blocked, then energy cannot flow freely. She says *chakras* are part of our 'subtle body' – one cannot see *chakras* with the naked eye, but we can feel their energy during meditation.

Susan patiently takes me through my seven *chakras*. She recommends books and teaches me *chakra* meditation to activate and release any blocks I may have, which I put into practice over the next few months. As I master the art of *chakra* meditation, I begin to feel more alert and energetic.

This also makes me think about how I was introduced to yoga a few years ago. I was sitting on the bus on my way to work and the woman in the seat in front was reading a health article in a Western women's magazine. The article had diagrams of yoga poses, which caught my interest. I bought the magazine on the way home and soon after joined a yoga class at the local community centre run by an English woman, Donna. After that, I developed a daily morning yoga practice which I added to the breathing techniques I learned while researching my thesis.

Another friend of mine, Maggie, is a member of the Western Buddhist Order. She encourages me to join her *Metta Bhavana* and Mindfulness groups. She explains that *'Metta Bhavana'* is the Buddhist meditative practice of cultivating loving-kindness toward all sentient beings. She tells me that it originates from India, that in Sanskrit, *'metta'* means *'love'*, *'kindness'* or *'friendliness'*, and *'bhavana'* means *'cultivation'*. This meditative practice can help to overcome hurt, bitterness, and anger toward others, as well as help develop self-love.

Maggie takes the *Metta Bhavana* group through the five steps of meditation. For the first step, she asks us to send unconditional love to ourselves and become aware of feelings of peace while meditating. Some of the group choose to repeat a loving phrase or well-wish for themselves. With step two, she instructs us to think of a close friend and their good qualities, repeating a loving phrase or well-wish for the friend. I do this for Jane, my best friend. The third step repeats the process, but for a person we have neutral feelings toward. I send this to an elderly gentleman that I often see walking past our house.

But I struggle with step four because we are asked to send love to a person we dislike. The rich boy at primary school surfaces in my thoughts and I notice I still feel resentful towards him so I work at directing love at him. In step five, we bring all these people together and then, while still repeating a loving phrase or well-wish, extend these feelings of loving-kindness to all people and things. In our discussion afterwards, I share the difficulty I felt with step four and the rich boy and Maggie tells me to sustain the practice until I am able to forgive him.

I enjoy the mindfulness sessions equally. Maggie explains that Mindfulness practices help individuals be more present – more aware internally of their thoughts, feelings, and physical body, and more aware externally of other people and the environment. She teaches us to cultivate a 'flow state' wherein we are fully immersed in an activity and giving it our total attention. She teaches us patience, which is something I know I have to make an effort with as I am known for my impatience in my family – I tend to get carried away with things I am passionate about and set myself unrealistic deadlines. She tells us when things unfold and happen at their own natural pace, it avoids the energy that is wasted by rushing in and expecting outcomes prematurely.

Maggie teaches us to be non-judgmental – impartial observers – and to let go of our habit of labelling what we experience as good, bad or neutral. By being more aware of these judgements, we can make more informed, conscious choices and be more accepting of all people from different perspectives and experiences. I recognise that Fai has taught me not to judge myself or others. She hardly ever gossips about anyone and only says things that are kind and helpful to others. She reinforces to me that nobody is perfect. Baa and Baapuji also brought us up to always see the good in others.

I love the sessions on mindful eating and walking. At work, I walk 'mindfully', aware of each foot as it meets the ground, as I go along the corridor from my office to the bathroom. My colleague is amused by my slow, purposeful steps and calls it 'the mindful walk to the loo'! I think of Baa in the mindful eating session. Maggie hands out some raisins and asks us first to eat them while talking to each other, and then to eat them silently, aware of all the sensations, taste, texture and temperature. When I was young, Baa used to take a vow of silence sometimes at mealtimes. I understand now she was doing this to engage fully in the eating experience and I am reminded again of how she said food was medicine for the body, how it had healing properties.

I also learn about 'The Beginner's Mind'. This attitude is best described by the behaviour of children as they view objects, people and experiences for the first time with intrigue and curiosity. I begin to look at things with fresh eyes, as if looking at them for the first time, and to let go of my preconceptions. I find this is easier said than done and forget to continue with this practice when not in group sessions.

But the best part is when Maggie takes us through the 'Three-Minute Meditation'. With eyes closed, she guides us:

'For this first minute, imagine a wide field of awareness both inside and outside of you. Notice your feelings and thoughts and the posture of your body. Notice the thoughts going round in your mind, observe them without judging. Detach from them and let them go...

'...In this second minute, bring your attention to your breathing and the gentle rise and fall of your abdomen. Without trying to change the way you are breathing, simply observe how your breath is flowing in and out of your body. If your attention wanders, gently bring it back to your breath, without judgment...

'...In this final minute, extend your sense of breathing to your toes and the top of your head and into your whole body. Visualise your whole body breathing through your skin. Tune in to the sense of wholeness and potential within yourself, fully surrendering to the beautiful, wonderful being that you are...

'Now slowly open your eyes and have a gentle stretch before you return to your everyday activities.'

I feel relaxed and calm and I thank Maggie for inviting me to these groups. Her sessions help me to reinforce some things I learned as a child and to learn some new concepts. I can add these to my repertoire of techniques that I began gathering at university. I realise it is easy to forget the simple habits that can make a powerful positive impact on one's life and I am grateful for the reminders.

***

DEEPAK CHOPRA CENTER, CALIFORNIA, USA, 2004

I am forty-nine now. After a gruelling journey, with a stop-over in New York, I arrive in Carlsbad, California, accompanied by my daughter who is now twenty-two. An English friend has lent me a book by Deepak Chopra entitled *The Seven Spiritual Laws of Success* and it has drawn me here, to his Center. I gather that his endeavour is to globally re-ignite the ancient Indian healing traditions, one of which is *'Ayurveda'*, and I have booked two spaces for his ten-day retreat on this subject.

Situated between San Diego and Los Angeles, the Center is positioned within a lush golf course adjacent to a health spa fit for the elite of American society. All the other delegates are Caucasian Americans. The staff teaching us *Ayurveda* and meditation are all Americans too. I was brought up in the Indian Ayurvedic health tradition, but completely lost sight of it when I came to England. Now, as a person of Indian origin, I am being brought back to my roots by Americans!

I learn that '*Ayurveda*' was developed in India more than three thousand years ago and is one of the world's oldest holistic ('whole-body') healing philosophies. It is based on the belief that health and wellness depend on a delicate balance between the mind, body, and spirit, and its main aim is to promote good health, not fight disease, though treatments can be geared toward specific health problems. It is explained to us that if the mind, body, and spirit are in harmony with universal energy, then good health is achieved, but when something disrupts this balance, it manifests as disease. Among the things that can upset this balance are diet, alcohol, genetic factors, injuries, climate and seasonal change, age, negative emotions, and stress.

Those who practice *Ayurveda* believe every person is made up of five basic elements found in the universe: space, air, fire, water, and earth. Our trainer, David, explains that these combine in the human body to form three life-forces, or energies, called '*doshas*', that control how the body works. These *doshas* are '*Vata*' (space and air), '*Pitta*' (fire and water), and '*Kapha*' (water and earth). Each one controls a different bodily function and everyone inherits a unique mix of the three, though one is usually stronger than the others. It is believed that the chances of getting sick and the health issues you develop are linked to the balance of your *doshas,* as well as the *chakras* Susan taught me about.

I learn that I am a *Kapha,* and my husband is a *Pitta. Ayurveda* has answered the question that has been lingering in my mind for thirty-three English winters: why am I always cold wearing a thick coat, scarves and gloves, when some people can walk past me in winter in only a shirt or a light coat? And finally my husband and I can settle the argument we have had throughout our married winters together: my constant *'Shut that window, please, I am cold'* commands when he leaves the windows open on chilly days!

My daughter and I have the *Panchakarma* treatments. We learn that *'Panchakarma'* is a Sanskrit word that means 'five actions' or 'five treatments'. The digestive processes which regulate the body's internal homeostasis often become disorganised as a result of disease and poor nutrition, dietary indiscretions, poor exercise patterns, lifestyle, and genetic predisposition, and *Panchakarma* is used to clean the body of toxic materials. We are taught that the process purifies the tissues at a very deep level through daily massages and oil baths, herbal enemas, and nasal administrations. The best part, we are told, is that *Panchakarma* treatments have been shown to create measurable brain wave coherence and to lower metabolic activity.

My daughter and I find the retreat a very pleasurable and relaxing experience. We enjoy the massages, yoga, meditation, Ayurvedic food, hymn-singing and other creative activities. By the end, I certainly feel stronger, am sleeping better, have improved concentration, clarity and focus, and enhanced creativity and greater confidence. The personal journey that my Western colleagues have started me on is more pleasant and relaxing than the one I went through in my university days. Both, however, have been instrumental in building my character, good health and personal empowerment. I can honestly say I feel like a new person.

***

Back in Birmingham, I give it my best shot at integrating these health and wellbeing philosophies into my routines and recognise I have simply reclaimed them from my childhood days.

I remember being ill as a child in Africa. I had a fever. Baa used damp cotton handkerchiefs soaked in salted water and laid on my forehead to draw out the heat of the fever. When one dried out, she would replace it with another damp one, until the fever receded. In those days, there was none of 'over-the-counter' medication that we have here in Britain. We only had one doctor in Thika who would be called upon only in dire emergencies. For all other health concerns, Baa used homemade herbal remedies and spiritual safeguards passed down by generations in India.

If one of us had a cold, Baa would say, '*Thandi vadhi gayi chhe, (Too much cold energy in the body)*' and give us concoctions of spices and herbs that would generate heat in the body to balance it out. If someone had a fever she would say, '*Garmi vadhi gayi chhe, (Too much heat in the body)*' and make a concoction to cool the body down. Her mantras and *kirtans* (spiritual songs) echoed through the house on most days, and she prayed and meditated in front of our little shrine at home daily, even with the constraints of raising a large family.

I tried to explain this to my British doctor a few times, but gave up and resigned myself to the use of prescribed medication during the early years in England. I do not necessarily have to do so now, thanks to the revival of my traditional healing practices in the western world.

CHAPTER 13

FOOD, MEDICINE, CARROT CAKE, AND VADAAS

BIRMINGHAM, ENGLAND, 2010

I am fifty-five years old now and, today, I am standing in an independent Asian grocery store figuring out the right food to buy to keep mine and my family's *doshas* balanced. Indian vegetarians eat all sorts of weird and wonderful vegetables rich in vitamins, minerals and protein, and I am trying to decide which to pick for this week's recipes. There is aubergine, *turiya* and *duthi* (two kinds of sweet gourd), *karela* (bitter gourd), *vaalor* and *guvaar* (varieties of runner beans), *saragvo* (a drumstick- shaped vegetable), and okra. There is also a range of greens and herbs: spinach, fenugreek, dill, coriander, mint and mustard. And there are British vegetables too: cauliflower, onions, potatoes of various varieties, cabbage and peas.

I just love fruit and nuts and have acquired the affectionate pet-name of 'Fruit-and-nut-case' from my work colleagues. My eyes wander off to the fruit section where there are all sorts of enticing, exotic, oriental fruits: mangoes, jackfruit, dragon fruit, star fruit, passion fruit, pineapples, guava and kumquats, as well as British varieties of apples and pears, European oranges, satsumas, and melons, and so on. It is hard to decide what to buy today.

I think back to my childhood when Baa had about five items to choose from Jerome's home-grown patch, whereas I have about fifty, albeit some artificially ripened en-route from various other parts of the world. As children, we looked forward to Baa sharing the bananas she had bought from Jerome – how we savoured and appreciated these little treats! With my children, I still have to persuade them to eat fruit and vegetables as part of a healthy diet and it's not uncommon to throw away overripe fruit that has not been consumed.

It's not *roti* for breakfast, lunch and dinner, any more, but all sorts: fish and chips, sandwiches, salads, pies, pizzas, burgers, bakes, stir-fries, fresh food, frozen food, takeaways, and food from all over the world. *'It is not always a good thing to have too much choice beyond the limits of one's requirements,'* I think to myself, and I feel sad at the waste of food when the leftovers are sent to landfills by households and supermarkets.

I wander off towards the counter of Indian savouries, mass-produced and packed in plastic wrappers. During my childhood, we made our own *poppadums* and savouries and the whole family got involved. I walk up to the next aisle. There is an enormous range of lentils, pulses, flours, oils, breads, and readymade savouries and sweets, mostly imported from all over the world. I am entertaining some friends this weekend and I want to make it a special evening for them.

Food is a universal language for the expression of love, and so much so in the Indian tradition. It is considered rude not to offer food to visitors or share a meal with them. For most Indians, it is natural to expect that a guest or visitor will share meals and be given food parcels at the end of their visit. When I first moved to the UK, I felt hurt when my British counterparts did not return my food gestures. It was only later that I understood this cultural difference.

This reminds me of Jane's carrot cake and I recall one of her visits when we are chatting in the living room.

'Oh... cake! I forgot all about the carrot cake that I brought for you.' Jane bolts up and scurries out to get the cake from her car. She knows we are all partial to her carrot cakes.

'Mmm... this is yummy. Thanks, Jane,' I say as I bite into a chunk. 'We do not have a family tradition of baking, we did not have an oven when I was growing up. To me, it is a very British thing. Back in Kenya, my mum cooked using coal in her *sagdi*. When we had guests and there was a lot of cooking to do, she would use a portable kerosene cooker. We used to call it a 'primus', but that must be a brand name – like the ones you take camping.'

I take another bite of the carrot cake and carry on,

'But I do remember making biscuits. My sister and I would help roll them out and cut them up with a small stainless-steel bowl. My mum would cook them on a griddle on her *sagdi* by covering them with a steel tray and piling more hot coals on top. Oh, yes, and she made *ondwo*, a savoury dish, the same way. I think you tasted it last year at the get-together we had in September... the yellow square cake like pieces with sesame on top... It was a special treat in those days and remains one of my favourites... Maybe you can teach me how you make this scrumptious carrot cake and I can show you how I make *ondwo* next time you come round?'

'That's a deal, Hansa. I would love that. Then I can show off my *ondwo* to impress my sister-in-law. She is a lover of Indian vegetarian food. She says as a vegan, Indian vegetarian food offers her a lot of variety and choice. She would love to meet you. And she'd be fascinated by all the varieties of pulses, lentils, cereals and flours in your pantry, and your fridge full of green vegetables and herbs that I had never seen before in my life.'

Jane suddenly bursts out laughing and I know why. I remind her, 'I made you eat that bitter gourd dish that you hated at first, but you finished all of it because I told you it is good for cleansing the blood. I can still remember that look on your face as you tried to swallow each bite.'

Jane responds, 'I didn't get around to telling you, but I introduced it to my mother-in-law because you said it was good for people with diabetes. She drinks its juice every morning and says she does not have to take her medication when she keeps up with it. If she can drink that raw, then I can eat a curry made out of it!' and howls with laughter again.

'Getting competitive with the mother-in-law, are we?' I tease.

'Shall we have some more cake and your special Indian *chai*?'

I go into the kitchen, get the aluminium *sufuriyu* that is put aside just for Indian *chai*, and fill it with two cups of water and a cup of milk. I then add three teaspoons of loose tea leaves and fresh ginger pieces, (in summer I would use cardamom pods), and let it heat up for a while. Once it comes to the boil, I leave it to simmer for a few more minutes.

'I know you don't take sugar in your English tea, but would you like it in your *chai*?' I shout to Jane from the kitchen.

'Just a bit, half a teaspoon,' she answers.

In the meantime, I put the teapot, strainer and mugs on a tray.

'Would you like some *vadaas* with your tea? ...The kind I brought to work on your birthday... I made them yesterday.'

'Of course! Why not? Can never have enough of your ve...dda... ss.'

Her pronunciation of '*vadaas*' amuses me. As I bring the tea and snacks into the living room, I say, 'It's va...daa, with a soft "D".'

'Vaa...dda,' she tries.

'No, soften the "D".'

'Va...daa,' she tries again, amid chuckles.

'Actually, there is a sound in the Indian spoken language that cannot be replicated with English phonetics. It is like a "n". In written English, it is replaced with a "D", "R", or "N", whatever the closest sound is. In the case of *"vadaas"*, the closest is "D".'

Jane has a few more attempts, and we have more howls of laughter.

Then I hear a *ping!* on my phone. It's Bhai. He is in Thika.

CHAPTER 14

COMING FULL CIRCLE

BIRMINGHAM, ENGLAND, FEBRUARY, 2018

I am sixty-two years old now. I am sitting in my study working on this book when my phone, usually turned off when I am working but I must have forgotten to do this today, pings. Bhai has just shared an article from the Thika local press.

Bhai is a member of The Thika Alumni Trust (TTAT), a group of former attendees of Chania Boys' High School now living in the UK who have joined together to raise money for infrastructural and educational improvements at our old school. Apparently, working with the school's principal and the *Kiambu County C.E.C. for Education ICT, Culture and Social Services*, TATT has just opened a new school e-learning centre. The school is piloting a ground-breaking technological platform developed by TATT called 'RACHEL' – *Remote Area Community Hotspot for Education and Learning* – a prototype offline digital repository for delivering free educational resources to developing communities. Because RACHEL is built as software and installable on any computer, it is ideal for communities without steady access to the internet, and the staff and students are palpably thrilled with the tools, skills, and opportunities this will provide for them to adapt to the increasingly global environment.

I think about Bhai there in Thika and wish I was there too.

My phone pings a few more times. Bhai has posted pictures of the school, the post office where Motabapuji worked, the debilitated grass square, the park in the centre of town, Motabaa's flat, the high street, and a few other spots.

I feel my heart ballooning and I text him:
Where is the picture of our house?

He texts back:
House has been demolished...
...New building being built there.

My heart shrinks and hits my stomach with a loud thud.

The house filled with eternal love; the house holding a million memories; the house where I and my siblings made an entry into this mysterious world; the house where I learned to make round *rotis*; the house where Baa would sing in her melodious tones as she went about her household tasks; the house where the perfume of the jasmine shrub wafted and lifted our spirits; the house where the courgette shrub took up proud ownership of the whole roof; the house where, on a Saturday night, Baa would sometimes fry scrumptious *bhajiyas* and Baapuji would have his occasional glass of beer and we would all sit and in a circle and share stories of our week; the house that sneaks into my dreams even now, is gone. The house that I will take my grandchildren to one day to show them my roots, they now will *never* ever see.

I stop writing.

I get up and make my way downstairs to where my shrine is. I sit down, cross my legs, and meditate. My mind goes off on a long wander. What kind of new building will it be? What history will the people who come to use have? Will there be love? Half an hour later, feeling more centred, I return to my office and start writing again.

***

A few weeks later, the house is in my dreams again. It is blurred, I cannot make out the people in it, but I recognise this feeling of grief. I meet it often in my work as a stress therapist. I think about some of the grief reactions that my clients have shared:

'It's as if I have lost an arm or a leg.'

'I feel empty, like there's a void inside me.'

'I feel as if there is a dark cloud over me.'

I reflect on what I know about loss but nothing makes sense. My grief is my grief, and everyone's grief is unique. I cannot say it feels like I have lost an arm or leg or I feel empty. To me, it feels as if there is a fracture in the deepest corner my soul. I will have to wait until it is healed by the sources of nature that make healing happen.

Something within urges me to go and visit my Fai. My busy schedule of working away from home, family, writing and singing means I do not do this often enough. But, you see, like the house, she is the last link to our family history, and it is the news of the house's demise that pulls me to her now. She is the last of Baapuji's siblings who crossed the vastness of three continents and who is still alive.

She is ninety-three years old, frail but still with the fighting spirit she has always had. Until a few years ago when she had a stroke, Fai would get her bag and coat and, scarf on her head, tuck her *saree* in tight and set off on the bus wherever she fancied. The British weather never put her off, even in coldest winter. I tell her I want to have her strength and courage in my old age.

I sit close to her on the sofa and we talk about Baa's final year with us before she recently passed away. I tell her that one day I was feeling unsettled about day-to-day things in life and I went to visit Baa. I sat down beside her, but, at this stage in her illness, she did not even recognise me. We had no meaningful conversation, we couldn't with her dementia, but, sitting in silence at her bedside, I nonetheless felt this inexplicable sense of comfort and safety. The muddle of problems in my head started to untangle itself and my tentative next steps gradually began to emerge. Baa's presence alone exuded the flow of acceptance and approval I was needing. To me, this is the power of unconditional love.

I tell my Fai I feel the same in her presence. I look at her still radiant, stunningly beautiful face. There is no look of regret or sorrow in it, but instead a look of serenity and contentment. I tell her while I have the chance, that she inspired me to believe in myself, to let go of fear, to do what I felt I needed to follow my true path and not worry about being judged by other people.

My siblings and cousins join us and we all begin to reminisce, knowing one day the opportunity will be lost to the family forever, I ask Fai about her memories of India and Kenya. This togetherness electrifies the atmosphere with the buzz of memories, support, care and love for one another. The house in Thika may be gone, but the love it contained is as strong as ever. And it keeps growing with every new addition to our family, with every new partner and child who has enveloped us and been enfolded by us in the same love and security we shared growing up. Even though Baa and Baapuji are now only with us in spirit, I find I have not felt an acute loss of them because their void has been filled by this love. As Fai's will also be one day.

BIRMINGHAM, ENGLAND, MARCH, 2018

I take a break from my writing, and put on the television to catch up with today's news. The snow and blizzards in Britain are the main story, Britain is having its worst weather in many years.

I recall my first experience of snow in England. It is everywhere: on the drooping branches of the trees, rooftops, cars, pavements, lampposts. I stand by the patio door for hours watching the soft flakes falling to the ground until the green of the grass and the grey of the patio eventually transform into a brilliant thick white carpet. It is pleasing to the eye, in fact very pleasing. When I venture out and lay the flats of my palm tentatively on it, my nerve endings race, jingling all the way to my brain. It is cold, squidgy, damp and soft, but very soothing to the touch.

I have fond memories of taking walks in the snow with my children and making snowmen, all of us in wellies up to our knees, our faces peeping out of the layers of warm clothing we are draped in. In the days of my equator sun, a thick winter coat, woolly hat and gloves were as alien to me as *turiya* curry and a pile of *rotis* would be to an Eskimo. But the kids squealing in delight on their snow sledges takes me back to my days in Thika when my brothers would push me on their homemade carts and I would let out the same high-pitched delighted squeal.

A question sneaks into my brain: seeing all this, have I missed my equator sun for the past forty-seven years of my life?

The answer is yes, and no. Yes, I miss it, but I have much more in its place now. I have the wonderful four seasons, which I love equally. I love the way the natural world and life change around the four seasons.

After the snow clears, the bare branches of my two blossom trees outside will sprout with young tender shoots. The daffodils will shine out in all their glorious shades of yellow. This sight always fills me with awe and I marvel as the sleepiness of winter begins to rouse and the world around me springs into life.

Then there is summer. The sight and feel of the sun, occasionally as fierce as my equator sun, throws the country into a frenzy. Everyone wants to make the most of it. Beaches and parks fill up. Barbecues are set up in gardens. Shorts and summer dresses get to leave the confines of wardrobes and go out on the bodies of sun-loving people.

Come September, the attire of the trees gradually changes from greens to yellows, mustards, deep reds, browns and terracottas until the leaves tumble to the ground.

We moan and groan as the cold of winter and dark nights descend on us again, but that is soon forgotten in the frenzy of Christmas – the season of goodwill and festivities.

In fact, for our family, the season of goodwill and festivities starts in late autumn during our Diwali celebrations. *Aarti* at the *mandir*, presents, a host of sweet and savoury foods, cards, family get-togethers, fireworks and the lighting of candles. Then there is a few weeks break and we start all over again, decorating the Christmas tree, cards, presents, Christmas lights, tinsel, Christmas pudding, and more family get-togethers.

Before you know it, it is the start of the New Year and another set of new beginnings is embraced. We are happy. We feel at home.

***

Talking of new beginnings, there's one that topples our world upside down and up again and sideways in all directions. One that gives us a tumultuous unleashing of new life in our veins. One that makes the world fade away to a backdrop. One that gives us another, altogether new, purpose and meaning to life...

The birth of my granddaughter in 2015.

CHAPTER 15

THE SHAPE OF THE FUTURE: A GLANCE INTO THE NEXT PHASE OF HISTORY

LONDON, UK, AUGUST 2018

My three-year-old granddaughter, Ana, has over thirty teddy bears and knows their names: Freddie, George, Shyam, Sima, Princess, Eon, Pinky, Ella the elephant, Snowy, Doggy, Horsie, and so on. It is a different world altogether she is growing up in.

I am sitting in the lounge of my son's house and it is half full of toys: building bricks, musical and educational toys, talking toys, a toy kitchen, toy cleaning set, toy golf set, a large toy car, a toy computer, toy kindle, toy mobile phone, toy-this and toy-that. There are loads of children's books too. And that's not all. The next room is half full of her stuff as well: car seat, buggy, pushchair, winter coat, summer coat, baby bike, baby scooter, box of disposable nappies, disposable baby changing mats, baby wipes.

And then there's upstairs where the nursery is full of yet more baby things.

I reflect on my days as a child. Not a single baby thing in sight in the house except for the homemade *ghodiyu* my siblings and I grew up in. Ah yes, and I must not forget the home-made nappies Baa made from old clothes. My own children had a handful of store-bought toys alongside their homemade ones. As a toddler, my son was happy to bang a wooden spoon on some plastic containers I had laid on the kitchen floor to keep him occupied and distracted while I cooked the dinner. He much preferred this to rattles and soft toys. As for my daughter, she preferred her handmade doll given to her by a relative over the expensive Barbie doll she got for her first birthday. I suspect present-day parents have a lot of peer and commercial pressure to have the latest toys and technical gadgets, which have a short user-span and yet take up lots more storage space in the house.

I watch Ana from across the room as she shuffles over to the sofa where all her teddies are lined up. She is looking adorable in her yellow jumper and navy dungarees, her hair tied in a bunch held by a yellow bauble. She has the makings of her mother's striking beauty: the creamy-milk complexion, the lotus-shaped lips, the silky hair. She emits a torrent of baby-talk and sweet laughter. Ana's laughter to my ears is like the chime of church bells. I chuckle to myself as I eavesdrop on her chattering to her teddies:

'Sham... Come and sit by Snowy. Do you want to go la...la...? Here, I shall wrap you with a blanket so you can go la la, aaahhh.'

She fumbles with a small blanket and clumsily pulls it over Shyam as she attempts to tuck him in, ready for bed.

'Now go to sleep, Shyam. Go la la,' she says a few times.

She looks up and notices I am watching her fondly. She runs up into my arms and into my embrace. I am touched by her innocence and I kiss her softly on her forehead. The embers in all the cells in my body come alive with a life of their own. A wave of joy cascades from somewhere in my heart down through the whole of my being, and I am reminded of the waterfalls of my ten-mile-radius world. It is like this every time my eyes fall on her.

'Ana, I love you,' I say to her.

I am not sure she would understand the unarticulated 'felt in the bones' kind of unconditional love I feel for her, that I was blessed to feel from Baa and Baapuji, but I feel blessed again to experience yet another manifestation of love and human connection.

Ana curls her little silky-smooth fingers to my wrist and beckons with the magic of her eyes. She has her father's eyes: curious, mischievous, playful.

'Freddie... Ta ta?... Freddie ta ta?' she pleads.

'No, Ana. Freddie cannot go ta ta yet. It is raining,' I say as I look up out through the patio-door.

It is supposed to be summer, but there is no hint of Baa's sky-blue *saree* shades beyond the billowing clouds outside, there are no rays of sun glinting like her golden bangles. The rustle of the rain is in league with the whistling wind as it pelts down on the patio tiles, neither with any intention of halting as yet, and I think of my equator sun. The patio-door is locked and there are stair rails to confine Ana to the living room, and I think of my beloved grass square in Thika. Niru and Sima surface in my mind's eye.

'Let's play *"Ringa, Ringa, Rosie"*,' I say to distract her.

She knows this from nursery so we ringa-ringa-rosie several times, falling on the carpet at every '*Aaaaatishoooo*'. Now that at least is something that has not changed, and I decide it is time to preserve the legacy of another.

***

Ana is sitting in her baby chair with her toy *patli* and *velan* and is being initiated on her culinary path. I show her how to hold the *velan* and how to roll the *roti* with a swirl of the hands and arms so that in time she will learn to make hot yummy *rotis* with the same rhythm that Baa did. I try to do this as well as keep the same rhythm with my *rotis,* but it does not work. Every few minutes, she demands that I give her a fresh piece of dough, and she wants my grown-up *velan*.

She has the same exuberant genes as my son. I can see for my son and his wife it may be like climbing Snowdonia as they grapple with the joys and jilts of parenthood. Working hard on their business, new house, the first grandchild in the family – they all take me back to my metaphorical climb to the top of Mount Kenya when I was raising my children.

But Ana loves to eat *rotis* and mild *turiya* curry, as well as *khichadi* and *kadhi*, and in her words expresses her enjoyment of these with a resounding, 'Yummy, yummy in Ana's tummy' while rubbing her dainty hands to her belly.

***

Since Ana has been born, a few topics have preoccupied me, and I keep coming back to one over-arching question: what does Baa's unconditional love and acceptance look like now, in this vastly different world to my ten-mile-radius Thika, and how do I demonstrate it to Ana? I know she is too young at the moment to comprehend this conundrum, but I can list my intentions for her and I hope I can start to sow the seeds as and when the opportunities arise.

Already Ana has got a toy phone and it makes me wonder how the digital revolution and the influx of social media will impact Ana and her generation.

'Ana... Let's do numbers. 1...2...3...' I call out to her.

'No, I .... call daddy, where's my mobile phone?'

She rummages through her toys until she finds the little pink plastic object, pretends to dial, and has a pretend two-way chat with her daddy. She paces around the lounge as she talks, having seen the adults do this.

'Daddy, what you doing, are you working? I played "Ringa Rosie" with Dama.' (She cannot pronounce 'dadima', meaning 'grandma', yet).

I side-track her and we manage a few numbers and animal names before her afternoon nap.

While she is napping, I think back to the simplicity of my childhood world devoid of gadgets and reflect further.

People seem more concerned about interacting with their mobile phones these days than asking someone how their inner world is. We are spending more time attending to the burgeoning technology in our houses than to real people. Delving into more and more screen time means we are neither alone, as we have hundreds of virtual friends, but not truly connected either. A sort of state of in-betweenness. This lack of connectedness and emotional expression leads to frustration and anger, as I see with my clients daily.

I wonder, do adults set the example of not really being there for their children when they are constantly glancing at their smartphones or texting and engaging in social media?

Luckily, both Ana's parents enjoy socialising and, despite their busy lives, make time for friends and family. They make a special effort to ensure Ana interacts with other children in their social network. I am glad they do this and at least still make phone calls, instead of texting, to maintain communication. But I wonder what it will be like for Ana as a mother in thirty years' time.

I observe that Ana is very lucky to have a lot of 'stuff', which is good in one way, and I hope she will give gratitude for the material abundance she is blessed with. But another viewpoint is that possessions do not make us better people or build inner strength and confidence. There is more joy in things we create than buy and discard in the current throw-away culture of excessive consumer choices. I hope for Ana to learn that possessions do not define our worth; that our worth is defined by how we interact with others.

I also notice children these days go from school to a multitude of different activities: gymnastics, piano, extra tuition, etc., and then come home where they have a rushed dinner so they can finish off their homework before going to bed and doing the same again the next day. Where is the time for rest and solitude? Is it any wonder that children sometimes end up anxious as adults? I believe life does not need to be faster, but more peaceful. Having regular time away in the quiet to make sense of the information overload and our experiences of the day is pertinent. In the absence of this downtime, frustration builds up and can lead to confusion and lack of direction. This is equally true of adults in our fast-paced culture.

On many fronts, there is the danger that we will lose connection with real people and with ourselves, and I conclude in the end that the answer is quite simple: unconditional love and acceptance are now, as they ever have been, about spending meaningful time together. They are about making space for emotional release and implicit permission to express oneself safely. They are about enhancing relationships and building a connected community rather than a competitive one.

Often, we are too engrossed in leaving a material inheritance to consider the ethical, moral and cultural legacy that fosters love and respect. Love does not necessarily need words. It can be expressed in actions, such as not making children feel they are a burden or a sacrifice, and showing them that they are your ultimate joy and pleasure and priority in life. Children sense our love as well as our distraction and resentment simply by the look in our eyes, by our expressions and daily actions. Children learn something from textbooks, but more from the examples and character modelled by the significant others around them.

This reminds me of another quote from Mahatma Gandhi:
'An ounce of practice is worth more than tons of teaching,'
And I recall Baa's words:
'Make a goal every day to be better than what you were the day before and keep a check on your moral compass all the time.'

Ana loves to join me when I do my early morning yoga. I wake up with her on the days I stay over so that my son and his wife can get a short lie-in and rest. I give her breakfast in the kitchen and we come through to the lounge. She likes to watch her Peppa Pig cartoon for a while. Then she lays her own yoga mat next to mine and mimics the moves I make. Some days it goes well and I manage to do an hour, but on playful mornings I may not even manage a few minutes. She will sit on me as I do my frog pose, or pull my legs as I do the cobra pose, before she goes back to her frolics. The same happens when I am meditating. She scrambles into my lap with her teddy and wants me to play with her. But this is our routine, and I hope to teach her yoga and meditation when she is old enough to do them.

Hopefully, I shall be able to inspire Ana, like Baa, Motabaa and my Fai, who guided me to tap into my strengths and be my own person. Just as I have been exposed to different cultures from birth, I wish Ana to learn about different cultures and be open-minded and curious about them. Her maternal grandmother loves gardening and nature so I can see Ana will be exposed to and be guided by her here. Hopefully, she will also be inspired to appreciate the natural beauty and goodness in people around her. Through our family, I hope she will come to understand that as humans we all have imperfections and weaknesses, but a simple gesture of love and tenderness can diffuse the anger and frustration they cause; that giving praise, admiration, gratitude, generosity and encouragement can be transforming.

***

Back in the kitchen, I am sweeping the floor with a *fagiyo*, clearing up the detritus of our *roti*-making lesson.

'Dama, I want the *fagiyo*.' Ana tries to grab it, she wants to do the sweeping.

It is hilarious watching her trying to manoeuvre the sweeps with a *fagiyo* three times her size.

'Look Ana, look by the door, there's a *"dudu"*.' I point to a small insect at the corner of the door leading to the garden.

Following my finger, she repeats like a parrot after me, 'Du... du... Dudu!'

Without being aware of it, I am passing on the Swahili language to her. It would never occur to me to call the *fagiyo* a broom or a *dudu* an insect, unless I am speaking to an English person.

She continues to persevere with the *fagiyo* with delight. I take a video and post it to our family WhatsApp group so we all can savour this moment of Dama-and-Ana fun. I love these moments.

***

Later that day, Ana is on the swings in the park. I am pushing her and she is in fits of laughter. Nearby, the church bells are ringing and I think of the bells at the *Mandir* in Thika.

'Whee!... Dama... Faster... Whee!... Faster!'

As the swing gathers momentum, I hear her squeals of joy, much sweeter than the sound of the church bells. I see the dazzling twinkle in her eyes, innocent gestures of her little arms and legs fluttering in motion to the rise and fall of the swing. And the ascent becomes effortless, with even more magnificent twists, tumbles and treasures to come.

I am very happy. I feel at home.

EPILOGUE BY
AN ANONYMOUS FRIEND

This is how we Indians grew up in Kenya! And what a life it was! We were innocent, frank and straight with people at home, at school and within the community and society. Our childhood was like an adventure, exploration, and expedition – an unassigned project to accomplish without the present-time luxuries, hi-fi tools, and unbelievable facilities, and with not so much help provided – no school loans, grants, financial aid or scholarships. Instead, it was filled with lots of fun, excitement, enthusiasm, trust, expectation, commitment and responsibility.

Although not so very easy always – and filled with some hardship – life was beautiful!

Our love and respect for our parents were second to none, and our respect for our teachers and elders in the community and society was in our genes. We gladly looked after our younger brothers and sisters without any selfish motive and fuss – we felt it was our prime and moral duty. We attended temples, *Gurudwaraas*, churches, mosques, *Jamat Khannas,* and prayed regularly and respected all religions.

We had mothers who did not check our blood pressure or temperatures every few minutes. We never saw or wore the present-time diapers, nappies and liners. We bounced ourselves without a bouncer and peacefully slept without a baby cot. We sucked cow's milk from a soda bottle without being sterilized or warmed in a bottle warmer. We slept during our sleep times be it day or night without monitors or bleepers. There were no nurses or doctors to pamper the mums, babies and children all the time.

Our baby cribs were covered with bright coloured lead-based paints. We had no childproof lids on medicine bottles, doors or cabinets. We rode our bikes without helmets, gloves and guards. As children, we would ride in cars that had no child-safety door-locks, seat-belts or airbags. Sometimes we sat on each other's laps for God's sake!

We ate raw mangoes with salt that set our teeth on edge, or a grilled *makaai* and *mogo,* and drank orange squash. We ate at roadside stalls, drank coconut water, yet we weren't overweight and falling sick because we were always outside playing freely and keeping fit, fine and happy. During holidays, we would leave home in the morning and play out all day, we were never ever 'bored' and were allowed freedom all day, as long as we were back home at a given time. We would dare not be late!

We were innovative and creative, making and building things from and out of the scraps and junk of old pram wheels and bicycle rims. We made kites from used newspapers, we played traditional games like '*Santa Kukdi*', and British games like Rounders. Luxury and things related to it were far beyond our imagination, expectation and reach. We were taught and groomed to be content with what we had.

We did not have Play-Stations, Nintendos, Xboxes, video games, no 99 channels on cable TV, no TV even, no video-tape movies, no surround-sound, no mobile phones, no desktop pc, no laptops, no iPods or iPads, no internet or internet chat-rooms, no hi-fi and Wi-fi. We just simply had a two or three-band radio placed in sitting room to be shared by all the family!

We did not have parents who would ask us questions like, 'What would you like to eat for breakfast, lunch or dinner?' We ate what was put in front of us. No menu, no choice, no fuss, no waste and no leftovers. After dinner every night in almost every household the school-going children would recite all the times-tables from one up to twenty-five before going to sleep!

We had very loving, caring and wonderful friends with loving parents whom we very fondly called 'Uncle' and 'Auntie', and we were not treated any different from their own children by them. We fell from the trees numerous times, got cut, hurt, bled, broke bones and teeth, and there were no compensation claims, but only the consolation to be strong, rise again and move on!

We ate fruit that had fallen on the ground, never washed them and yet never got sick! We used to bathe using a bucket, and *Lifebuoy* soap. We did not know what shampoo, conditioner or a bath and body wash were. We rode bicycles everywhere in the town with someone sitting on the carrier or crossbar – to school, cinema or playgrounds. We knocked on the door of a friend's house and were welcomed without any hesitation and would be treated with some goodies!

This generation of ours has produced some of the best risk-takers, problem-solvers, inventors, winners, and most successful people ever. The past fifty years have been an explosion of innovation and new ideas, with some failures, but mostly successes. We had patience, understanding, discipline, respect, maturity, wisdom, motivation, commitment and responsibility.

And above all: we learned and survived the hard way, with our parents and grandparents overseeing us with their experience, guidance and blessings!

MESSAGE TO MY FUTURE GENERATIONS

I feel blessed that my children are happy at home in Britain. Their history will be quite different from mine. Hopefully, someday, they will have their own sagas of unconditional love and connectedness that they will share with the world. My hope is that my children and their future generations will make an extraordinary mark on history by giving back to their country, people and the planet. My hope is that they will do this in whatever fields they and their peers are excelling in.

Everyone has a special gift that they are born with and I hope my children will use this for the good of this amazing planet. My thirst for making a difference is not quenched by any measures, nor do I hope theirs will be. By giving back to people and planet, I do not mean give back in tiny droplets, but make it rain, and even better if it turns into thunderstorms that refresh and nourish the land that blessed them with liberalism and opportunities.

I hope I have conveyed in this book this central message: that regardless of country and culture, the most important factor for the survival of a healthy and happy person, after their basic physical needs, is the need for psychological safety and total love and acceptance as a human being. We do not need collective splits of 'I am Indian, Kenyan or English,' but rather, to come together as a humanitarian community. Personal splits cause mental health issues and collective splits cause war, destruction and discrimination.

I wish with my heart that my future generations will capitalise on their inheritance of these family values, thirst for education, and flair for entrepreneurship to make this a better and peaceful world for all living beings.

GLOSSARY OF GUJERATI AND SWAHILI WORDS

FAMILY

Gujaratis, unlike Westerners, do not use the blanket term of uncle and aunt for all parents' siblings. Mother's side and father's side have different terms of address.

Baa – Mother. Originates from North West Indian province of Gujarat

Baapuji – Father

Bhai – Brother

Fai- Father's Sister

Motabaa – how one addresses the wife of a father's older brother, meaning 'Big Mother'

Motabapuji – how one addresses a father's older brother, meaning 'Big Father'

SPIRITUAL

Aarti – An inseparable part of Hindu worship rituals. This ritual is said to descend from the ancient Hindu Vedic Fire Rituals. The word '*aarti*' comes from '*aa*' which means '*complete*' and '*rati*' which means '*love*'. It is not only limited to God but performed to all forms of life, inanimate objects, and people to invoke love and blessings.

Gurduwara – Sikh Temple

Maharaj – A Hindu priest

Mandir – Hindu Temple

Mantra – A group of words that impart positive and healing energy

FOOD

Kenyan

Bhoga- Fresh vegetables

Irio – Corn and kidney beans cooked with potato and spinach

Mogo – African yam, also called cassava

Sukuma Wiki – A combination of chopped leafy-green vegetables that is fried with onions and tomatoes and seasoned with salt and pepper.

Ugali – A cornflour dish cooked with milk and water to a firm consistency

Indian

Bhajiya – Vegetable fritters, a cross between vegetable tempura and *pakora*

Garam garam – 'Piping hot'

Kadhi – Yoghurt soup

Khichari – A dish made of boiled rice and lentils

Ondwo – A baked savoury dish made with soaked ground rice, chickpeas, yoghurt, and spices

Roti – Chapati

Rotlo – Millet, barley, or corn flatbreads

Sambharo – Sautéed carrots, cabbage, and green chillies

Siro – A dessert made from semolina

Turiya – A ridged green gourd eaten as a vegetable

Vadaa – A flat two-inch-round spicy savoury made from millet or cornmeal (or both) flour, fried. The Keralan (south of India) version of a *vadaa* is different.

DRESS

Kikoys – A traditional wraparound worn by men along the East African coast and inland

Kitenge – An African textile, typical of the Swahili tradition, used in Tanzania, Kenya, Somalia, as well as in many other African countries. It is a long rectangular piece of cotton fabric, wax-printed, commonly used for making skirts, dresses, shirts and fittings.

Salwar Kameez – Attire for women from South East Asia. *Salwar* is a trouser and *Kameez* is a long hip-length shirt of varying styles.

Saree – A female garment from the Indian subcontinent that consists of a drape varying in length, from five to nine yards, and two to four feet in breadth, that is typically wrapped around the waist, with one end draped over the shoulder, baring the midriff. There are various styles of manufacture and draping.

Shervani- Long embroided shirt worn by men on special occasions

MISCELLANEOUS

Bwana – Swahili term meaning 'Sir'

Dudu – Swahili for 'insect'

Fagiyo – Swahili for 'broom', typically a long bunch of dried shoots secured at the top

Ghodiyu – A homemade cot that is like a hammock, a piece of rectangle fabric attached to four hooks on a wooden stand, used as a cot.

Goma – A traditional African dance

Patli – A flat board, about ten inches across, with small knobs at the bottom on which *rotis* are rolled.

Patlo / Patla (singular / plural) – A two- to three-inch-high, flat stool for sitting on the floor.

Sagdi – A round mini-barbecue. Coal is put through a little opening in a round metal container topped by mesh and a stand where you place pots when cooking.

Santa Kukdi- A game of Hide and Seek.

Sufariyu – Swahili for 'cooking pot'

Sumuni – Five cents in Kenyan currency when I was a child.

Tabla – An Indian percussion instrument like a drum.

Tavdi – A round metal or clay griddle

Velan – A rolling pin, thicker in the middle and tapering out, used for rolling *rotis*.

ALSO BY
HANSA PANKHANIA

**FROM STRESS TO SUCCESS – FIVE INSPIRATIONAL STORIES
TO OVERCOME WORKPLACE STRESS**

In her first book, Hansa draws on her extensive experience of
working as a Stress and Well-being Consultant with individuals and
groups in private, public and voluntary sectors. The stories are
inspired by her day-to-day work and contain powerful messages
and simple coping strategies in five different areas: stress
management, resilience building, anger management, mediation,
and change management.

**STRESS TO SUCCESS IN 28 DAYS – A DYNAMIC PROGRAMME
FOR TOTAL WELLBEING**

In her second book, Hansa brings together all the tools and
techniques for wellbeing and stress reduction that she has
accumulated over her twenty-year career and skilfully presents

them in a twenty-eight-day programme that any individual, employee, or manager can easily integrate into their day-to-day routine.

STRESS TO SUCCESS STORIES – TO INSPIRE MANAGERS AND EMPLOYEES TO EXCEL

In her third book, Hansa shares simple, powerful techniques that will help you to live a stress-free, healthy, and energetic life, as well as optimise effectiveness and productivity within any large organisational environment. Demonstrated through artful storytelling, these techniques are a unique blend of Eastern and Western influences and philosophies.

All books and audio are available on Amazon and through her company website: **www.aumconsultancy.co.uk**

The aim of Hansa's books is to reach out and make a positive difference to people's lives. Any feedback to help her to do this better is appreciated. Please feel free to leave a review of the books on the website or Amazon.

ACKNOWLEDGEMENTS

My gratitude to my family for their unending love and support for my projects is evident from the content of this book.

My heartfelt thanks to the Solihull Writers' Group for their encouragement, especially Maureen Blewitt and Robert Ferguson for their support.

Also to Carla Halford, Jackie Jones, Norma Bayliss, Mina Parmar, Bina Shah, Nalini Rajpara, Karen Swanne, Ros Powell, Jacqueline Howell, Claire Prosser, Zen Kyle, and Pat Maier for their inspiration – they all speak to me from their hearts.

Also to author A. A. Abbott for her time and support, and my editor, Nina Abbott-Barish, for imparting her expertise and wisdom.

And lastly but not least, to The Higher Being, for the guidance and strength to follow my true path.

ABOUT THE AUTHOR

Hansa Pankhania was born a British citizen to parents of Indian origin in Thika, a small town in the British Colony of Kenya. She is an author, speaker, coach and trainer. She has written several books on Stress Management and Wellbeing. She is a Fellow of the International Stress Management Association and Director of AUM Consultancy. She lives in the UK with her husband, children, and grand-children.

For more information, visit: www.aumconsultancy.co.uk

CPSIA information can be obtained
at www.ICGtesting.com
Printed in the USA
BVHW072129120223
658291BV00015B/2197